Alien
OBSESSION

Ron Rhodes

HARVEST HOUSE PUBLISHERS
Eugene, Oregon 97402

Cover design by DesignTeam, Grand Rapids, MI.

ALIEN OBSESSION
Copyright © 1998 by Ron Rhodes
Published by Harvest House Publishers
Eugene, Oregon 97402

Library of Congress Cataloging-in-Publication Data

Rhodes, Ron.
    Alien obsession / Ron Rhodes.
        p.   cm.
    Includes bibliographic references.
    ISBN 1-56507-849-7
    1. Occultism—Controversial literature.   2. Unidentified flying objects—Religious aspects—Christianity.   3. Parapsychology— Controversial literature.   4. New Age movement—Controversial literature.   5. Experience (Religion)—Controversial literature.
I. Title.
BR115.03R48   1998
261.5'13—dc21
                                                                97–44911
                                                                CIP

98 99 00 01 02 03 04 / BC / 10 9 8 7 6 5 4 3 2 1

To all the faithful supporters of
REASONING FROM THE SCRIPTURES MINISTRIES

Acknowledgments

I want to thank my wife, Kerri, and my two children, David and Kylie, for their continual support and encouragement during the writing of this book. Without them my work of ministry would truly be an impossible task.

Contents

Have We Been Visited?

Something does seem to be happening out there. And it seems to be increasing in frequency as humankind presses toward the year A.D. 2000.

> —William Alnor, Christian
> UFO Researcher[1]

They have landed!"

With these startling words, broadcast coast to coast on Halloween Eve in 1938, the United States was hurled into a frenzied hysteria. Radio personality Orson Welles was reading from H. G. Wells's book *War of the Worlds* as if it were actually taking place.

Toward the end of the program Mr. Welles, in the character of Professor Richard Pearson, a famous astronomer, intoned: "As I set down these notes on paper, I'm obsessed by the thought that I may be the last living man on Earth."[2]

Neither Welles nor anyone affiliated with the radio broadcast had even the slightest idea that the citizens of the United States would turn on their radios and actually believe they were in the midst of a horrific invasion by aliens from outer space.[3] It was an insane evening. And it marked the beginning of an ongoing fascination with UFOs and alien visitations for the American public.

Almost every civilization that has kept a written history has recorded the sighting of strange objects and lights in the skies.[4] In modern times UFOs have been spotted by the likes of former President Jimmy Carter and a number of American astronauts, reportedly including those who participated in the Apollo 11, Apollo 12, Gemini 7, Gemini 11, and Skylab 3 missions.[5] (In December 1965, for example, Gemini astronauts James Lovell and Frank Borman claimed to have seen what appeared to be a UFO while making their second orbit of Earth.[6]) Such seemingly credible sightings have caused many to wonder if earth is truly being visited by aliens from another planet.

The modern UFO era began in the late 1940s—just a few years after the Orson Welles broadcast—when people all around the globe began reporting flying saucers whizzing across the sky at incredible speeds. In the 1950s some people (considered as being on the "fringe") claimed to be "contactees" for alien civilizations somewhere within our own solar system.

The 1970s and '80s witnessed increasing numbers of people in the United States and around the globe claiming to have been *abducted* by aliens. These stories made headlines in some of the nation's most prominent newspapers. Then, in the late 1980s, UFO enthusiasts began finding a new respectability as the New Age movement grew in popularity and influence.[7] Today UFOs are a virtual craze.

Just What Is a UFO?

The word "UFO" refers to an unidentified flying object. We must keep that definition in mind. These objects, whatever they are and wherever they come from, are indeed *unidentified*, their origin unknown.

The best scientifically accepted definition of a UFO is probably that provided by the late astronomer J. Allen Hynek, who said that a UFO involves—

> the reported perception of an object or light seen in the sky or upon the land the appearance, trajectory, general dynamic, and luminescent behavior of which do not suggest a logical, conventional explanation and which is not only mystifying to the original percipients but remains unidentified after close scrutiny of all available evidence by persons who are technically capable of making a common sense identification, if one is possible.[8]

UFOs are typically described as being circular or spherical in shape with flashing lights and luminous brilliance. They are often said to change color and shape. They appear and disappear suddenly, seeming to defy the laws of science. According to the testimony of many UFO enthusiasts, UFOs can in a mere matter of seconds accelerate to speeds of several thousand miles per hour, and make 90-degree turns in midair.[9] Such maneuvers are obviously quite beyond anything known to man.

J. Allen Hynek, for over 20 years the Air Force's astronomy consultant to *Project Blue Book* (a government-sponsored UFO investigation),[10] came up with a well-known system of categorizing encounters with UFOs. He suggested two broad categories—*Section One* (the most common sightings) and *Section Two* (close encounters)—with three major subcategories under each of these.

Section One Categories (Most Common Sightings)

1. *Nocturnal lights.* This type of "sighting" involves strange lights that one might see in the sky from a distance.

Unusual features often accompany the sighting, such as variations in the intensity of light and color, and incredible and sudden changes of speed and direction.

2. *Daylight disks.* This type of sighting involves seeing a distant disklike object in the sky during the daytime hours.

3. *Radar/visuals.* This type of sighting involves two simultaneous aspects—a visual appearance of an object in the sky *and* radar confirmation. Such "sightings" are very rare.

Section Two Categories (Close Encounters)

Hynek suggested that there are three types of close encounters.

1. *Close encounters of the first kind* are those "in which the reported UFO is seen at close range but there is no interaction with the environment (other than trauma on the part of the observer)."[11]

2. *Close encounters of the second kind* are similar to the first except that there are physical effects on both animate and inanimate objects.

> Vegetation is often reported as having been pressed down, burned, or scorched; tree branches are reported broken; animals are frightened, sometimes to the extent of physically injuring themselves in their fright. Inanimate objects, most often vehicles, are reported as becoming momentarily disabled, their engines killed, radios stopped, and headlights dimmed or extinguished. In such cases the vehicles reportedly return to normal operation after the UFO has left the scene.[12]

3. *Close encounters of the third kind* are those in which occupants (aliens) of the UFO craft are reported in or around the craft.[13] Hynek generally ruled out "contactee" cases in which

a person claimed to have had intelligent communication with the "occupants," arguing that such reports were almost invariably made by pseudoreligious fanatics and never by "ostensibly sensible, rational and reputable persons."[14]

Some time later, UFOlogists suggested another subcategory—*close encounters of the fourth kind*—to cover cases in which humans are allegedly abducted by extraterrestrials. Emergency medical physician Steven Greer of Asheville, North Carolina, came up with yet another category: *close encounters of the fifth kind,* in which humans and aliens intentionally communicate through ordinary light and sound.[15]

In the following chapters of this book I will touch on each of these kinds of encounters in greater detail. I should tell you right up front that I don't believe we are actually being visited by aliens from outer space. As will become clear throughout the book, I believe that all UFO sightings can be explained as involving one of the following:

1. *Natural phenomena,* such as weather balloons or satellites, being mistaken as UFOs.

2. *Deliberate hoaxes,* such as those involving obviously doctored photographs.

3. *Demonic spirits* impersonating "space brothers." (Generally occultic phenomena are present in such cases.)

Were the Ancients Visited?

By now almost everyone has heard of the theories of Erich Von Daniken to the effect that aliens visited Earth in ancient times. His book *Chariots of the Gods* summarized these theories and quickly became a bestseller on an international level. Since the publication of his book, Von Daniken's theories have been regurgitated and scrutinized in numerous publications. In an article entitled "God Versus the Flying Saucers" by scholar Carl Pfluger, we find the following summary of how Von Daniken sees things:

These aliens, according to our UFOric prophet [Erich Von Daniken], descended upon early humans (or upon prehuman anthropoids—he's not very clear about such fine points), raised the level of their intelligence by a bit of genetic tinkering (or perhaps merely by interbreeding with them), taught them the rudiments of civilization (giving them also a glimpse of space travel and a whiff of nuclear weaponry), and finally flew off as abruptly as they had come; whereupon people [such as the Nazcas], abandoned and pining for the return of their celestial mentors, built "landing strips" and imitation spacecraft (the Pyramids and such, you know) in order to lure them back to Earth . . . . Traditional religions and mythologies clearly bear witness to these events [such as the carvings of astronauts by the Mayans], says Von Daniken, who asks, with charming simplicity, why else should all religions locate their gods up in the sky?[16]

Some of Von Daniken's speculative conclusions hardly call for a response. However, we might note the opinion of scholars who have studied ancient cultures that while some ancient Mayan carved figures might remotely look like an astronaut, the reality is that these figures portray masked Mayans dressed for their religious rituals. One scholar informs us that "masks with exaggerated features of symbolic significance are common among tribal people all over the world, and there is no reason to assume that they necessarily are representations of extraterrestrial beings."[17]

As for the alleged landing fields for spaceships constructed by the Nazcas, it is far more likely that the Nazcas believed that the gods were up there in the sky. Among other factors, it hardly seems likely that a race advanced enough for interstellar space travel would need such feeble landing strips in order to touch down on Earth. Surely their crafts would be more sophisticated than that. Moreover, as one scholar has pointed out, the Nazcas—

> could see the Sun God rise in the morning, and the Moon God come out at night, and hear the Thunder Gods when they were angry during a storm, flashing their weapons in the sky. It is reasonable that the Nazcas might want to send messages by making big drawings in the sand that the gods above could see easily, such as: "Send more rain, and while you're at it, drop a few stiff lightning bolts down on our enemies over there." Some of the same motifs, probably part of important rituals, are found on Nazca pottery.[18]

There is certainly much more that could be said in responding to Erich Von Daniken. (Indeed, Von Daniken says UFOs are in the Bible, and I'll talk about that later.) It is sufficient at this point to simply note that other scholars have more than adequately debunked Von Daniken's speculations.

A Growing Paranoia

Christian UFO researcher William Alnor, while recognizing that there is a legitimate and much-needed side to UFO research, once commented: "I also found that the UFO arena is loaded with fakery, hoaxes, and people so paranoid they probably belong in mental institutions."[19] I came across this paranoia often in my own research.

For example, some people have claimed that the aliens are involved in genetic experiments on certain human beings with a view to making communication between aliens and humans easier. Others claim that U.S. government leaders have made a secret deal with the aliens, allowing them to abduct and run experiments on unwary humans in exchange for high technology.

Some believe the government has known about the aliens for a very long time and will one day make all this known to the world. In fact, some in the UFO movement believe we are rapidly approaching a time they call "full global disclosure," during which the U.S. government will announce the existence of extraterrestrials, or perhaps state that there has been communication with alien intelligence.[20]

More recently some people have speculated that our "stealth" airplanes—the Lockheed F-117 stealth fighter and the Northrop B-2 stealth bomber—have benefited from "outside" assistance.[21] Still others have claimed that some of today's "superchips" being used in the computer industry were derived from aliens.

Further, there has been great controversy about cattle mutilations that have been discovered all over the world. Typically the body of the animal victim has been totally drained of blood. There is no sign of struggle. There are no human footprints or tire tracks near the scene of the crime. In many cases the owners of the cattle heard nothing on the night of the mutilation. Often the tongue is removed with a precise incision deep in the throat. An eyeball is often cut out, as are the sexual organs—again with surgical precision. Why the mutilations? Some UFO enthusiasts say that the answer may lie in the fact that cattle blood is similar to human blood. Perhaps the UFO aliens are studying the cattle in order to find out more about us.[22] (A more likely explanation is that satanic cults are engaging in these mutilations for their blood sacrifices to Satan.)[23]

And then there are the crop circles. Many believe these circles are caused by the landing of UFO spacecrafts. British New Age author Benjamin Creme says the crop circles are definitely formed by "UFOs manned by the Space Brothers," and their purpose is to alert humankind that the New Age is upon us. "This is a time when highly evolved beings are moving into the world, in every nation and country, giving experiences to people, showing them a higher life, a higher wisdom."[24] (Many researchers, however, have provided convincing evidence that deliberate hoax is involved in all crop circle occurrences.[25])

Regardless of such speculation and paranoia, the good news, we are told, is that today one can purchase a genuine $10 million insurance policy against alien abductions, which comes with a gold-bordered policy suitable for framing. The bad news is that the claim form "requires the signature of an authorized on-board alien."[26]

Funny!

Ted Daniels, editor of the *Millennial Prophecy Report,* says that a company in London is now offering insurance against inadvertent intergalactic pregnancy if one is 1) abducted and sexually molested by an alien space invader, and 2) thereby impregnated.[27]

In this book I intend to examine in some detail UFOs, aliens, making contact, the controversial subject of abductions, and more. In the process I will explore the *curious,* the *bizarre,* and in some cases the *unexplainable.* The goal throughout is to come to a biblical understanding of the "aliens" and their agenda.

1

UFOria:
The Wild Popularity of UFOs

We're in a major alien moment.
—Newsweek magazine[1]

In the 1940s people did not take UFOs too seriously. A 1947 Gallup poll found that "virtually no one considered the objects [UFOs] to be from outer space."[2] Most people considered such sightings to be either hoaxes, secret weapons, illusions of some kind, or some phenomenon that could be scientifically explained.[3]

By the 1950s a slight shift in public opinion became evident: 3.4 percent of the population now believed in UFOs manned by extraterrestrials.[4] By 1973, 11 percent of Americans claimed to have seen a UFO.[5]

By 1987, according to a Gallup poll, some 50 percent of Americans believed in the existence of UFOs—the same percentage that considered extraterrestrials to be real.[6] One in 11 people (about 9 percent) reported that they had seen something they thought was a UFO.[7]

Then, by 1990, some 14 percent of Americans claimed to

have seen a UFO.[8] And today, because of the ever-increasing popularity and growth of the New Age movement, Americans are more open than ever to the idea that our planet is being visited by extraterrestrials.[9]

A 1997 poll indicated that 45 percent of a thousand people surveyed said they believed unidentified flying objects have visited the Earth in some form, and 48 percent thought UFOs were "something real." About 12 percent said they had seen something they thought was a UFO, and a full 71 percent believed that the U.S. government knew more about the phenomenon than it has publicly revealed.[10]

Still another poll indicated that 31 percent of Americans believe that a spacecraft from another planet crashed in Roswell, New Mexico, in 1947. Some 38 percent believe "there are people somewhat like ourselves living on other planets."[11]

A Space Invasion

Today it would seem that America is in the midst of a space invasion. In fact, because of the statistics just listed, *Newsweek* magazine concluded that "we're in a major alien moment."[12] On every front we witness indications of people's fascination with outer space and the possibility of extraterrestrial life.

During the time it took me to write this book, the Pathfinder landed on Mars. There was life-threatening trouble on the Mir space station, which made headlines everywhere. There were tragic suicides of the Heaven's Gate cult, which believed that an alien "mothership" was coming in behind the Hale-Bopp comet to pick them up. Among the top movies released were *Men in Black* (the Fourth of July's top film) and *Contact,* based on a novel by the late Carl Sagan. On television the top-rated shows include *The X-Files* and *Third Rock from the Sun.* "God made so many wonderful beings that it's foolish to think we're the only ones out there," says *Third Rock's*

Simbi Khali, who plays Nina, assistant to John Lithgow's Dick Solomon.[13]

Also during the time it took me to write this book, there was a 50-year reunion of sorts at Roswell, New Mexico. People from all across the country came to participate. Showtime even produced a special docudrama on the Roswell phenomenon. (As I'll detail a little later in the book, many people are convinced that a UFO did in fact crash in Roswell, New Mexico, in 1947.) Actor Martin Sheen commented on the Roswell incident, saying: "I wish it were true. I really do. I'd love there to be ETs—as long as they were better creatures than we are."[14]

In a *Time* magazine article entitled "Do Stars Believe in UFOs?" we read that "the entertainment industry seems to have aliens on the brain," citing the already-mentioned *X-Files* and *Third Rock from the Sun.*[15] The article notes that "Jackie Gleason was enough of a UFO fan that he built a country house in the shape of a saucer and called it the Mother Ship."[16]

In my earlier years I was involved in the entertainment industry and had the opportunity to appear on *The Dinah Shore Show* with my brothers and sisters. Jackie Gleason suddenly showed up at the television studio, and found himself on the show as well. I distinctly remember Gleason talking about how he owned one of the largest private collections of occult books in the world. We will see later in this book that there is a very definite connection between occultism and the UFO phenomenon.

Capitalizing on this fascination with space, in recent years there have been many alien-themed advertisements on television. In fact, I've seen such ads from the likes of Kodak, Hostess, Quisp Cereal, Volkswagen, and Breathe-Right nasal strips.[17]

Presently some 300 academics in the United States are studying UFOs.[18] And over the past five decades, at least a thousand books—ranging from vanity publications to those from major publishing houses—have been written on the subject in the United States alone.[19] Many of these are still in print. In fact, according to *Books in Print,* currently there are nearly as many books available about UFOs (256) as there are about the Kennedy family (266), who without doubt represent the "gold standard" when it comes to public interest in a subject.[20]

UFO-themed magazines and journals include *Journal of UFO Studies* and the *International UFO Reporter.*[21] Another key publication, *Unicus—The Magazine for Earthbound Extraterrestrials,* boasts of having 3 million subscribers.[22] I came across one New Age magazine, *New Frontier,* that ran a "dirt for sale" advertisement—selling dirt that had allegedly been supercharged by extraterrestrials. It stated: "UFO landing site radiates cosmic energy, alters psychic awareness. Soil samples $5."[23]

The question is, Why have UFOs become so popular in recent years? What has happened in our culture for "aliens" to have touched such a nerve with the American public? Why are we so *obsessed* with this phenomenon?

I think there are a number of factors involved. I will suggest three of the more important factors that have led to the current UFO craze, although certainly there are other factors besides these three that have contributed to UFO interest, and we'll touch on some of these throughout the rest of the book. But these three factors represent a foundational starting point for all that follows.

People *Want* to Believe

First, it would seem that many Americans *want* to believe in extraterrestrials. As one UFO investigator put it, "There's something about human nature that wants to believe in flying saucers and extraterrestrial life."[24]

John Wiley, in *The Smithsonian*, commented, "Many people, I suspect, want the aliens to arrive for the sheer excitement and for the disruption of the routine of daily life."[25] Indeed, Wiley says:

> We have a history of yearning for alien life. The popular response today to movies about lovable, or at least benign, aliens seems little different from the excitement of newspaper readers in 1835 over a phony report that Sir John F. W. Herschel had "discovered" batlike people living on the moon.... The hoax could not have lasted as long as it did unless people wanted to believe it.[26]

Psychologists say that some people have an actual *need* to believe. They note that a belief in something grand fills a void in people's lives and gives them something to hold on to. In a way, it comforts them and gives perspective to their daily toil on this old Earth.[27] One UFO enthusiast said, "I want to believe. I think, deep down, we all want to. Knowing for a fact that it's true would send a chill down my spine."[28]

UFOs Give Us Hope

Another reason suggested by UFO enthusiasts for the popularity of UFOs is that they give people a sense of hope in what often seems to be a hopeless world. As one psychologist put it, "Many flying saucer buffs are believers precisely because aliens may offer hope, much like a deity." Indeed, "Americans are desperately searching for hope in an increasingly cynical age."[29]

It is certainly no coincidence that UFOs and aliens are becoming more prevalent and popular in an age when humanity seems to need help from the beyond to solve such ills as homelessness, hunger, the destruction of the environment, and out-of-control crime. "We as a human race have not been able to solve our own problems," one UFO enthusiast mused. "People have been looking outside the human race for help. Some people turn toward God. Some people who don't believe in God are going to turn toward something else."[30] That "something else," for many people, comprises the UFOs.

The screenwriter for the blockbuster movie *Men in Black*, Ed Solomon, agrees, noting that "Earth as a planet is suffering from the view that the grass is greener on the other side of the intergalactic fence. I think people are looking above and beyond for things to find hope in . . . ."[31] People today are lost in the machinery of society and are getting chewed up by it. They have a need for someone they can trust—a "space brother" who will watch out for them in this threatening world.

It is my belief that this turning to benevolent aliens for help during troubled times parallels what we see happening in the massive angel movement, with people turning to "celestial helpers" during times of trouble (see my book *Angels Among Us: Separating Truth from Fiction*). It is highly revealing that in a feature article on angels, the *Los Angeles Times* reported that "times have gotten so bad that guardian angels are turning up in individuals' lives with increasing frequency, and people are more receptive to the heavenly beings than ever before."[32]

In *Do You Have a Guardian Angel?* John Ronner says that tough times have helped increase interest in guardian angels. "We're in somewhat troubled times now . . . . People find a great deal of comfort in the thought that something larger than themselves and benevolent may be looking out for them."[33]

"People need protection, and they're scared," says Rabbi Susan Laemmle of the University of Southern California Hillel Center. "The world is a dangerous place, and anything we can do that will give us a sense of protection is attractive."[34] Many people feel insecure because of rising crime and seemingly insurmountable societal problems, and they believe they have found a means of coping by trusting in guardian angels. The same is true in regard to trusting in "space brothers." Some people are turning to *celestial* helpers; others are turning to *extraterrestrial* helpers. They're turning everywhere but to the one true source of comfort—the God of all comfort (2 Corinthians 1:3).

UFOs Can Help Fill Our Spiritual Need

Many astute observers of our society have noted that the popularity of UFOs cannot be divorced from the spiritual hunger that pervades this country. Humans are by nature religious. God created people with an innate desire to find spiritual answers to life's deeper questions—to seek a "higher source" outside of the human experience. When people find these answers in the Person of Jesus Christ, the resulting relationship is healthy, both emotionally and spiritually.

Unfortunately, many people today are turning to UFOs and extraterrestrials to fulfill this spiritual need. Roswell, the site of an alleged UFO crash, is a phenomenon that "clearly fills a need. UFOs, many commentators now argue, ride the airwaves and the distribution channels out to a spiritually needy nation."[35]

One observer of the times said that the present popularity of UFOs "indicates a hunger—it's a hunger for contact, for communication with something larger than humanity. I think there is very little reasoning going on because the belief need is so high. *The need to believe.* It's a religious kind of impulse, I think."[36]

Author Keith Thompson suggests that we are in a time where traditional "religious myths" have fallen short: "The '60s and '70s opened up a lot of spiritual hunger. There has been a kind of shift in consciousness and a greater openness to psychic phenomena,"[37] including psychic phenomena related to UFOs.

Herbert "Hub" Corn is one of those who claims that humans had contact with aliens some 50 years ago in Roswell. "I get dadgum goose bumps every time I come here," says Corn, a sheep rancher who once was a skeptic but now believes in UFOs. "[I believe] it came skidding across the desert there, bounced down that hill, then smacked into this cliff."[38] Like millions of people who believe in things that can't be proved, Corn finds an almost spiritual comfort at the cliff, where he feels what he calls a "connection" not just to extraterrestrials but to "something a whole lot bigger . . . things I can't explain."[39]

Again, I believe that this spiritual hunger and yearning that is so evident in the current UFO movement is also reflected in the angel craze over the past decade. Joan Wester Anderson, author of *Where Angels Walk*, says that angels are a "gateway to spirituality." Popular angel writer Eileen Freeman agrees, and notes:

> Many adults find modern views of God unacceptable or too impersonal, too distant, and do not accept the Christian view that Jesus is God in human, personal, accessible form. The search for God is a part of our inmost being. The need to be united with our Source is universal. It is, as Blaise Pascal the French philosopher put it, the "God-shaped vacuum in the center of every human heart." Such people often see in angels what they cannot yet see in God: personal love reaching out to touch them; ageless wisdom reaching out to enlighten them; incredible power harnessed to inspire them.

As it is with angels, so it is with these "space brothers" aboard UFOs. People sense some kind of spiritual connection with them. And for those who have turned from the God of Christianity, the void in the human heart sucks in counterfeit spiritualities—such as angel helpers or extraterrestrial space brothers who are here to enlighten us.

Men of words have often noted man's intrinsic need for the transcendent. Allan Bloom, for example, finds evidence for a longing for the transcendent on our university campuses today.[40] Charles Colson, in his book *Kingdoms in Conflict*, declares that human beings "desperately long to know the Power beyond us and discover a transcendent purpose for living."[41] Anglican theologian John Stott proclaims that "without transcendence, the person shrivels . . . . Ecclesiastes demonstrates the meaninglessness of a life that is imprisoned within time and space."[42] Both angels *and* extraterrestrials give people a sense that they have come into contact with the transcendent.

There are certainly other reasons for the growing popularity of UFOs, and we'll touch on some of these throughout the rest of the book. In the next chapter, however, we will turn our attention to a foundational issue—the search for extraterrestrial life in the universe.

2

The Search for Extraterrestrial Life

What is at stake in the search for extraterrestrial intelligence is nothing less than our understanding of what it means to be human.

—Frank White, *The SETI Factor*[1]

The question as to whether there is extraterrestrial life in the universe has been debated from the beginning of recorded history. There are even records from the fifth century before Christ indicating man's interest in the subject.[2] Democritus (460–370 B.C.), Epicurus (341–270 B.C.), and Lucretius (98–54 B.C.), for example, believed there were other worlds inhabited by life. Others, such as Aristotle (384–322 B.C.), said there is no life on other planets. The debate continues to the present day.[3]

Current polls indicate that 72 percent of Americans believe there is life in some form elsewhere in the universe. And some 38 percent believe people somewhat like ourselves live elsewhere in the universe.[4]

Hugh Downs, host of the ABC news program *20/20*, is among those who believe there is life out there:

It's overwhelmingly unlikely that we are the only intelligent beings in the whole shebang, and I find myself hoping we'll get some proof that they're out there (and friendly). But so far, in spite of discovering conditions that make extraterrestrial life more likely, there are no credible signs of extraterrestrial intelligence. Maybe tomorrow.[5]

In the past many scientists have been skeptical about the possibility of life on other planets because of the precise conditions necessary for the development and survival of lifeforms. It was argued that planets that are too small cannot retain an atmosphere. And without an atmosphere of oxygen, the chemical reactions that allow cells to extract energy from other chemicals cannot run. Planets that are too hot or too cold have no liquid water. And without water, the chemical process known as photosynthesis (a process that converts sunlight into energy) is not possible.

Today, however, those who argue for the possibility of life on other planets generally point to the fact that there are conceivably millions of earthlike planets out there in each of billions of galaxies. Hence, it is reasoned, surely some of those planets must be inhabited by life-forms like us.[6] As the late science fiction writer Isaac Asimov put it:

> If we cling to the optimistic view, then on any planet very much like earth, chemical changes would have taken place similar to those which took place here. Life would form; but even if it formed on the same chemical basis, no one could tell how it would appear structurally. Yet some alien life-forms might develop intelligence, and that intelligence, at least, might resemble ours. The chances of such intelligence developing can only

be speculated upon. However, if intelligence developed only one time in every million life-bearing planets, there might be over 600 different types of intelligent beings in our galaxy alone.[7]

Sometimes those who argue *against* the possibility of life on other planets (especially for religious reasons) find themselves on the receiving end of cutting remarks. The (Christian) Institute for Creation Research (ICR), for example, once put out a statement that said:

> To date there is not one iota of real evidence in either science or the Bible that intelligent beings were either evolved or created anywhere in the universe except on earth. In any case, it is the planet earth which is the focal point of God's interest in the universe. There is no need to look, because there couldn't be anyone out there.[8]

Whitley Strieber, who claims to have been abducted by aliens and who documented his experience in the best-selling book *Communion*, responded to ICR by saying, "The banality of this position makes it more pitiful than frightening."[9]

Not Just Christians

Though Strieber doesn't want to hear about it, it is not just some Christians who doubt the existence of life on other planets. For example, Dr. Frank Tipler, a professor at Tulane University, is convinced that there are no intelligent beings other than humans that have developed in the Milky Way galaxy. "If the Martian evidence holds up," he says, "we may have to face the fact that *primitive* life is common in the universe but that the development of *intelligence* is vastly improbable. I believe we are the very first intelligence to arise in our galaxy."[10]

Other scientists believe there is intelligent life out there in the universe, but for some reason these advanced life-forms have not communicated with us. Several hypotheses have been suggested. Some hold to the "self-destruction hypothesis," which says that there have been advanced civilizations out in space, but they blew themselves up or committed suicide before they were able to travel to other planets.

Others hold to the "contemplation hypothesis." This theory holds that "mature civilizations grow out of the adolescent urge to colonize, preferring to stay home and explore the frontiers of art or contemplate the meaning of life."[11]

Or it may be that there are advanced life-forms out there but they are *so far away* that it is impossible for them to reach us. Doctor Seth Shostak—one of the world's leading physicists and astronomers, and director of the SETI ["Search for ExtraTerrestrial Intelligence"] Institute in Mountain View, California—is among those who say there are millions of aliens out there but they are just too far away. They may be so advanced that human beings would be like insects or rodents to them.[12]

Shostak believes that our first contact with an advanced civilization will be with some sort of self-replicating machine created by the aliens. Let's face the reality, he says, that the nearest extraterrestrial life is very far away. In fact, in order to reach the nearest solar system which could support life, it would take more than 100 years traveling at a speed of 40,000 miles *per second.*[13] Not an easy task!

In view of this, Shostak says, our first visitor will likely be an intelligent machine, capable of rebuilding itself and making clones to launch off to other missions. This machine "will be programmed to expect an encounter with another civilization and will make efforts to communicate with us while analyzing our strengths and weaknesses," Shostak speculates.[14]

SETI: The Search for ExtraTerrestrial Intelligence

SETI stands for Search for ExtraTerrestrial Intelligence. This organization seeks to detect evidence of technological civilizations that may exist on planets orbiting other stars. Potentially, it is suggested, there are billions of locations outside our solar system that may contain life. It is SETI's purpose to find some of these locations.[15]

In the popular movie *Contact*, starring Jodie Foster, scientists are portrayed hunting for extraterrestrial life using powerful radio telescopes. Like their Hollywood counterparts, the scientists at SETI use such telescopes to listen for evidence of alien life out there. SETI scientists listen for signals between 1000 and 3000 megahertz on the radio dial, where natural background static is at a minimum. After weeding out earthly and satellite signals, they have so far come up empty. There have been no messages from space. But they keep listening.

For a time SETI enjoyed government funding. But Congress trimmed the budget and in 1993 SETI ended up on the monetary cutting floor. Since then, the efforts of SETI have been sustained (with an annual budget of $4 million) through private contributions.[16]

Among those supporting SETI is Hollywood motion picture mogul Steven Spielberg. At a special SETI ceremony Spielberg, accompanied by his son Max, made the following comments:

> Well, I'm very happy to be involved in this project because, as you all know, I've benefited so much from science fiction, I just thought it was time to get involved in science reality. And I'm real happy today to be here. And I guess everybody always considers space as a new frontier. I still think there are so many problems at home, that has to remain

the frontier. But for Max's generation, when Max grows up, hopefully, he'll be the recipient of some outstanding information which the project will give. Something like, well, we're all the same.[17]

A reporter asked Spielberg if he thought there was life out there.

"Yes, absolutely," Spielberg replied. "The question is, is there life here? Especially, *intelligent* life?" Everyone laughed.[18]

Since SETI became privately funded, the organization has been perpetually involved in surveying 1000 stars that are similar to our sun (and hence more likely to support planets capable of hosting life) but are many light-years away. They hope that this survey—code-named "Project Phoenix"—will help answer the age-old question: *Are we alone in this great big universe?*

Project Phoenix involves a massive effort to detect extraterrestrial civilizations by listening for radio signals that are either being deliberately beamed our way or are inadvertently transmitted from another planet.[19] Because millions of radio channels are monitored simultaneously by Phoenix, most of the actual "listening" is done by computers.[20] By mid-1996 Phoenix had examined approximately one-third of the stars on its "hit list." So far—*nothing.*[21]

Some have suggested that there may be a major kink in Project Phoenix. What if these extraterrestrials do not use the same electromagnetic spectrum as human beings do? The aliens may be so technologically advanced that electromagnetic waves are like a stone and chisel to them. They may be talking up a storm right in our faces and we don't realize it because our primitive equipment can't hear it.[22]

Other people have constructed a number of possible scenarios if there ends up being no response to SETI efforts. For example, it could be there will be no contact because:

1. No one is there.
2. The extraterrestrials are beyond the search-space that SETI is exploring.
3. The techniques being used by SETI are all wrong.
4. The extraterrestrials are not in a communicative phase.
5. The extraterrestrials are seeking to avoid us.[23]

We could debate such scenarios for days on end. The bottom line at this point is that a phenomenal amount of money has been spent listening for the slightest hint of the existence of alien life-forms, and it has been all for naught thus far. But the scientists at SETI are still hopeful.

Religious Implications of First Contact

A great deal has been written by secularists in recent years regarding the religious implications of "first contact." The question is, How would the major organized religions of the world (not just Christianity) react to the discovery that there really is life on other planets?

Certainly the various New Age religions would rejoice, for they already believe in "space brothers" who seek to help us.[24] Tibetan Buddhists as well would rejoice, for, as the Dalai Lama said, "We Buddhists have always held that firm conviction that there exists life and civilizations on other planets in the many systems of the universe, and some of them are so highly developed that they are superior to our own . . . ."[25] But what about the *other* religions? How would they react?

Don Berliner and Stanton T. Friedman, in their popular and controversial book *Crash at Corona: The U.S. Military Retrieval and Cover-up of a UFO,* ask:

> What if the aliens practice a religion closely resembling one familiar religion and thus reject all the

others? Or if they practice a religion bearing absolutely no similarity to any of Earth's major or minor religions, and thus reject all of ours? Or if their lives include nothing that bears the slightest resemblance to religion at all, and thus reject the very idea of religion and of a supreme being? For that matter, what if they had gone through a period of Earthlike religious behavior and then passed it to a nonreligious life that clearly suited them better?[26]

Would the religions of the world immediately seek to proselytize the aliens and try to persuade them to a new point of view? Would there be some sort of an intergalactic religious war? Berliner and Friedman reflect:

> The aliens' attitudes toward Earth religions would almost certainly be a very upsetting experience for hundreds of millions of people around the world who had been taught from childhood that theirs is the only true faith of the universe. If these obviously advanced beings function well without a recognizable deity, the need for religion as we know it would be diluted if not eliminated.[27]

The late astronomer Carl Sagan believed that religious groups which hold that man is the pinnacle of God's creation (*Christians*) are the ones who will have the greatest faith-struggle when contact is made with aliens:

> There are some religious groups that hold tightly to the view that we are the pinnacle of creation, that there are no other intelligent mortals, and there is nothing in the Bible about other civilizations . . . . Those sects that believe human beings are the

pinnacle of the mortal fraction of creation are going to dislike this [alien contact] a whole lot. [28]

The book *First Contact: The Search for Extraterrestrial Intelligence* echoes the sentiments of Sagan, emphasizing that man as an evolved being is really nothing special:

> Contact would tend to confirm the theory that life evolves chemically from inanimate matter, through universal processes, implying that there are other alien civilizations in addition to the one we had detected. We might see ourselves as just one example of biocosmic processes, one facet of the Universe becoming aware of itself. We would undergo a revolution in the way that we conceive our own position in the Universe; any remaining pretense of centrality or a special role, any belief that we are a chosen species would be dashed forever, completing the process begun by Copernicus four centuries ago.[29]

In view of the above, one can at least understand why some Christian pastors in the United States have speculated (mind-boggling though it may seem) that one goal of Satan as we draw deeper into the end times may be to supernaturally stage or mimic an actual landing of an "alien" spacecraft,[30] or perhaps supernaturally broadcast a message to earth from "aliens" in deep space. Later in the book we will look at evidence that these "aliens" are in fact demonic impostors. At this juncture, it is enough to make note of this possible stratagem of Satan. For if Satan were able to pull off this feat (Scripture indicates he has the power to produce counterfeit signs and wonders—2 Thessalonians 2:9), he would no doubt make a strong argument through the "aliens" *for* humanistic evolution and *against* Christianity.

Finding Meaning in Contact?

Many people in our day believe that coming into contact with aliens would actually bring meaning to the human race. Frank White in the book *The SETI Factor* says: "What is at stake in the search for extraterrestrial intelligence is nothing less than our understanding of what it means to be human."[31] Never mind what the Bible says! If only we can encounter alien life-forms, we are told, we will finally understand our humanity.

Carl Sagan is another writer who at least indirectly indicated that meaning may be found in alien contact. I am referring to the hit movie *Contact,* which was based on the novel by Sagan. After seeing the movie, Brooks Alexander of the Spiritual Counterfeits Project commented to some fellow Christian apologists who attended the movie with him, "Sagan, a man who spent a career systematically stripping the evidence of God from the cosmos, was now attempting to regraft purpose and meaning into it."[32]

Alexander pondered that in Sagan's heart of hearts, man's existential dilemma—the harshness of his utter aloneness in a seemingly infinite universe—was too much to bear. So Sagan "found solace in the idea that there were other lonely, purposeless beings out there who shared our predicament. By contacting these fellow denizens of the vast, irrational, impersonal cosmos, we would find some 'meaning.'"[33]

True meaning, of course, can only be found in a relationship with the living God, something that Sagan always missed (see Psalm 1). Indeed, "standing in denial of his connection with God, Sagan looked for 'connectedness' in his fantasies of alien life. It's a pathetic substitute."[34]

Religious Implications of *Not* Making Contact

Are there any religious implications of *not* making contact with extraterrestrials? Many would say yes. One religious implication, some suggest, is that the lack of alien life would seem to confirm religious teachings that man is unique. As Frank White put it, "Religious people would point out that we are not really alone in the universe, because God . . . is still there and always has been." Indeed, "Finding that there are no other intelligent life forms simply confirms religious views of humans as special and unique."[35]

Or perhaps the lack of alien contact would confirm a more *pantheistic* ("all is God") view of the universe:

> [We would discover that] the millions of life forms on Earth . . . are connected to us in subtle and substantial ways. We are part of a web of life that is mysterious and beautiful; we should spend more time searching for terrestrial intelligence, which includes not only ourselves, but the entire biosphere and perhaps the planet itself.[36]

Isaac Asimov, when asked about the religious implications of a lack of alien contact, made quite an admission, coming from an avowed humanist and atheist:

> There could be a new kind of loneliness and desolation, developing a fear of a vast impersonal universe in which we are lost. The other side of the coin is that we could begin to appreciate the uniqueness and preciousness of Earth, and save it not only as our home, but as the only home of an intelligent species in the entire universe . . . . Another reaction might be to prove that Earth is a special creation. It might create an enormous religious revival.[37]

Perhaps the humanist Asimov, in a weak moment, hit upon a truth in his old age. For indeed, the Earth *is* a special creation, according to the Genesis account (Genesis 1,2). And man created upon this Earth *is* the pinnacle of God's creation (Genesis 1:26,27). Let us now turn to a Christian perspective on the question of life on other planets.

A Christian Perspective

Christian thinkers have found themselves on both sides of this issue, some of them arguing *for* the possibility of life on other planets and others arguing *against* the possibility. Billy Graham once commented, "I firmly believe there are intelligent beings like us far away in space who worship God.... But we would have nothing to fear from these people. Like us, they are God's creation."[38]

Some who argue for the possibility of life on other planets point us to John 14:2, where we read: "In my Father's house are many rooms; if it were not so, I would have told you. I am going there to prepare a place for you." The reference to the "many rooms" in the Father's house, it is argued, allows for the possibility that life-forms from all over the universe will live with redeemed humans in the Father's house. Christians who argue against the possibility of life on other planets say this is "eisogesis"—that is, reading a meaning into the biblical text that is not really there. In context, it is argued, the verse has only to do with redeemed human beings, not aliens around the universe.

Certainly God has the power to create life on millions of planets throughout the universe if He wants to. However, though not being dogmatic about it, many theologians have noted that there are several good reasons that point to the likelihood of there *not* being intelligent life on other planets.

First, though atheistic scientists would scoff at this, Scripture does in fact point to the centrality of planet Earth and gives no hint that life exists elsewhere. As I point out in my book *Christ Before the Manger: The Life and Times of the Preincarnate Christ*:

Relatively speaking, the Earth is but an astronomical atom among the whirling constellations, only a tiny speck of dust among the ocean of stars and planets in the universe. To the naturalistic astronomer, the Earth is but one of many planets in our small solar system, all of which are in orbit around the sun. But Planet Earth is nevertheless the center of God's work of salvation in the universe. *On it* the Highest presents Himself in solemn covenants and Divine appearances; *on it* the Son of God became man; *on it* stood the cross of the Redeemer of the world; and *on it*—though indeed on the New Earth, yet still on the earth—will be at last the throne of God and the Lamb (Revelation 21:1,2; 22:3).

The centrality of the Earth is also evident in the creation account, for God created the Earth *before* He created the rest of the planets and stars . . . . Why did God create the sun, moon, and stars on the fourth day rather than the first day? One possible explanation is that in this way God has emphasized the supreme importance of the Earth among all astronomical bodies in the universe. In spite of its comparative smallness of size, even among the nine planets, to say nothing of the stars themselves, it is nonetheless absolutely unique in God's eternal purposes.[39]

Why the Vastness?

One might ask why God would create such a vast universe of stars and galaxies if He did not intend to populate them. Psalm 19:1-4 gives us the answer:

The heavens declare the glory of God;
the skies proclaim the work of his hands.
Day after day they pour forth speech;
night after night they display knowledge.
There is no speech or language where their voice
is not heard.
Their voice goes out into all the earth, their
words to the ends of the world.

The sheer vastness of the physical universe points us to the greater vastness and infinity of God Himself.[40] By observing nature, we can detect something of God's existence and discern something of His divine power and glory. We might say that the whole universe is God's "kindergarten" to teach us the ABCs of the reality of God.

The great French theologian John Calvin once said:

Men cannot open their eyes without being compelled to see God. Upon his individual works he has engraved unmistakable marks of his glory. This skillful ordering of the universe is for us a sort of mirror in which we can contemplate God, who is otherwise invisible.[41]

This then is why God created so many stars and planets—not to inhabit them with multiple life-forms but to serve as a testimony to His power and glory. It is not necessary to argue that simply because many planets exist in the universe on which life *could* exist, life *does* therefore exist on those planets.

Related to the issue of possible life on other planets is the question of how unfallen beings (assuming the "aliens" did not "fall" into sin on their planet) could share the same universe with fallen ones (humans who did sin). One

Christian apologist responds to this question by pointing out that—

> the effects of Adam's sin seem to pervade the entire universe (Romans 8:19-22). (I believe the second law of thermodynamics—that all things tend toward disorganization and death—is the scientific description of the curse God pronounced on creation in Genesis 3:14-19.) It does not seem likely that God would allow the effects of sin to impact a world of unfallen creatures (e.g., Revelation 21:4).[42]

Certainly there is room for debate within the family of God on the issue of whether life exists on other planets. We should not divide from other Christians on this issue. But in view of these factors, it seems to me that from a theological perspective there is good reason to say that there is no intelligent life on other planets.

Of course, if this is the case, any discussion of Earth being visited by extraterrestrials from other planets is rendered moot. But if *there is* some kind of "alien" message received from deep space in the coming years, I urge Christians to be discerning and beware of the wiles of the devil (Ephesians 6:11), who is pulling out his "biggest guns" to deceive people with counterfeit signs and wonders as we continue to move into the end times, the last days of planet Earth (2 Thessalonians 2:9).

——— 3 ———

What Really Happened at Roswell?

I'm sure I saw those aliens.
—Frank Kaufmann, retired government agent[1]

In the blockbuster movie *Independence Day,* there is a scene aboard Air Force One in which the President says to the character played by Judd Hirsch, "Regardless of what you may have read in the tabloids, there have never been any spacecraft recovered by the government. Take my word for it. There's no Area 51. There's no recovered spaceship."

One of the President's advisers then says, "Excuse me, Mr. President, that's not entirely accurate."[2]

This scene is rooted in the Roswell incident.

"Air Force Captures Flying Saucer on Ranch in Roswell Region." That headline appeared in the *Roswell Daily Record* on July 8, 1947, during the nation's first wave of UFO sightings.

Some 50 years ago, *something* crashed in the desert of Roswell, New Mexico—but exactly *what* crashed has been in dispute ever since. On that fateful July 8, Roswell Army Air Field announced it found the remains of what it called a "flying disk" (which made newspaper headlines the following

43

morning, not just in Roswell but around the world). The wreckage was rushed to the Army Air Command in Fort Worth, and Fort Worth authorities quickly recanted the flying saucer report, suggesting instead that the wreckage was part of a weather balloon.

For nearly 50 years believers in extraterrestrial life have searched for clues to what *really* landed in Roswell.[3] Of particular interest to many is whether alien bodies were discovered at the crash site. Roswell eyewitnesses say yes; the government says no. The controversy continues.

The Roswell incident is truly the cornerstone of UFO lore. References to this crash in the desert—and a government conspiracy to conceal evidence of extraterrestrial astronauts—abound in books, magazines, TV shows, motion pictures, and pulp fiction. TV episodes of *The X-Files* and *Dark Skies,* for example, have mentioned the Roswell incident. And Showtime produced its *Roswell* docudrama in 1994.

While on a state visit to Ireland, President Bill Clinton made the following comments during a speech in Belfast:

> I got a letter from 13-year-old Ryan from Belfast. Now, Ryan, if you're out in the crowd tonight, here's the answer to your question. No, as far as I know, an alien spacecraft did not crash in Roswell, New Mexico, in 1947 [*pause for laughter, according to an official transcript*]. And, Ryan, if the United States Air Force did recover alien bodies, they didn't tell me about it either, and I want to know [*applause*].[4]

The Incredible Popularity of Roswell

The polls reveal that a huge segment of the American population are believers in a Roswell UFO crash. A Time-Yankelovich poll revealed that 65 percent of Americans polled think a UFO crashed at Roswell.[5] A poll conducted by *USA Today,* CNN News, and Gallup sampled 1013 adults nationwide and came up with a much-reduced figure: Only 31 percent believe an alien spacecraft crashed at Roswell in 1947.[6] Whichever poll is closer to the truth, between one-third and two-thirds of Americans think a UFO crashed at Roswell, and that's a lot of people.

Roswell, New Mexico, has always been popular among UFO enthusiasts. But in July of 1997 Roswell celebrated its 50-year anniversary, and the whole world became fascinated all over again with the Roswell phenomenon. The UFO incident has proved to be the city's main source of income, not only during the anniversary year, but every year since the crash. (Roswell has benefited to the tune of $5 million per year in tourism.)[7]

A UFO convention organizer in Roswell said, "We weren't lucky enough to have, you know, a beach or a great mountain setting or anything else, so we have to go with what we've got. And we had a UFO crash."[8] During the 1997 anniversary in Roswell more than 40,000 people trekked to the city to celebrate at "ground zero" of UFO mania. Every hotel and motel room was booked for 70 miles in every direction. Restaurants had to double their staffs. Prior to the onslaught, local news programs advised residents to be sure to visit the grocery store to stock up on food.[9]

During this time of celebration the options were seemingly endless in terms of souvenirs and memorabilia. One booth offered alien abduction insurance. Another booth offered an alien Artificial Insemination Kit.[10] One vendor advertised intergalactic passports, which may work for travel outside the universe, but weren't guaranteed to solve passport problems when traveling inside the European community.

Local residents cashed in on Roswell's fame by selling

alien dolls, alien T-shirts, alien cookies, alien water, alien caps, alien jewelry, alien phone cards, alien balloons, alien quilts, alien bumper stickers (one said, "Crash in Roswell Tonight"), and Frisbees decorated with skinny, light-skinned, four-fingered aliens with bulbous heads and huge eyes.

One vendor had brisk sales of alien Slime. For $2.49 you could buy 3 ½ ounces of slime that bounces and stretches. It also came in a variety of colors.

Another vendor was selling alien embryos. The six-inch embryos—made from liquid plastic urethane—floated in jars containing orange or green liquid.[11] Yes, it's gross, but the kids loved it.

The New Mexico lottery even got into the act, selling $1 scratch-off tickets called "UFO Dough." Lottery officials were careful to point out that they were not endorsing an alien landing.

The U.S. Postal Service also got into the festive spirit. The service designed and sold $5 commemorative envelopes decorated with a cartooned green alien in a silver spaceship—equipped with a steering wheel—with flames of fire shooting out the bottom in wavering lines that spell out "50."[12]

All in all, the Roswell celebration was a huge financial success for the community. "All those people came to town and bought all the UFO paraphernalia, but they also bought gasoline, motel rooms and food," said Roswell Mayor Tom Jennings. "It was a real boost for our community."[13] Jennings mused, "Something happened here and it's probably the most credible UFO event in the world. We've taken that and developed it into a whole new industry—tourism."

Individual Roswell citizens also prospered in a variety of ways. The Roswell Jaycees, for example, ran a UFO trade exposition, renting $150 booths and charging $1 admission. The group netted a whopping $20,000—money that is being used to fund college scholarships for two Roswell teens.

Local churches in Roswell used the celebration as an evangelistic opportunity. A sign outside of one church said, "Jesus is the only alien who died for you." Another church had a sign that said, "He didn't leave in a UFO, He's not returning in a mothership, but He is coming back in glory." One pastor commented that the festival is "an opportunity. These people are looking for something."[14]

The Press Release That Started the Controversy

It is beyond the scope of a single chapter to examine in detail the myriad of details related to the Roswell incident. (Whole books have been written on this topic.[15]) We can, however, sketch a broad picture of what happened.

We begin with the fact that Walter Haut, Air Force press officer during the time of the Roswell affair, holds to his story to the present day that he was ordered by a Colonel William Blanchard to issue the press release that started the never-ending controversy. Now 75 years old, Haut says he distinctly remembers Blanchard saying, "We have in our possession a flying saucer. This thing crashed north of Roswell, and we've shipped it all to General Ramey, 8th Air Force at Fort Worth."[16] A press release was issued, and by the next morning the story had spread like wildfire.

The initial furor was short-lived, however. Just a few hours later a general at the regional Army Air Force command in Fort Worth, Texas, where the debris had been sent for further analysis, announced that what had really been recovered was a weather balloon.

> At 8th Air Force headquarters . . . Brigadier General Roger Ramey, after consultations with his weather forecaster, Warrant Officer Irving Newton, called in the local press and announced that the debris was the remnants not of a saucer but of

a high-altitude weather balloon. The sticks and
tinfoil, he explained, were from a reflector used to
track the balloon by radar.[17]

Hence the Roswell controversy, in its initial form, can be
reduced to this: Either a UFO crashed and the government
covered it up, or the crash was that of a simple weather balloon—nothing more and nothing less. There have been numerous people on both sides of the controversy for decades.

Since 1947 the Air Force has continually denied that it
recovered a UFO spacecraft or alien bodies. In a 1994 report
Air Force officials asserted that, upon further investigation, the
debris recovered outside Roswell in July 1947 has been found
to be the remnants of an Air Force balloon (not a *weather* balloon) used in a top-secret project that monitored the atmosphere for Soviet nuclear tests. But not addressed in the 1994
report was a second key element of the Roswell incident: Were
alien bodies removed from the site and carted off to a military
hospital?

In a 1997 Air Force report entitled "The Roswell Incident: Case Closed," officials indicated that those alleged
"aliens" were actually "anthropomorphic" (manlike) test dummies that were carried aloft by U.S. Air Force high-altitude balloons for scientific research. These dummies—which had
skeletons of aluminum or steel, skin of latex or plastic, cast
aluminum skulls, and instrument cavities in their torsos and
heads—were parachuted to earth from 1954 to 1959 as experiments that explored possible ways for pilots or astronauts to
safely return to Earth from high-altitude missions.

The report then suggests that the Roswell eyewitnesses
have confused memories of events that are nearly a decade
apart (the parachute experiments took place from 1954 to
1959, while the Roswell incident took place in 1947). The
"eyewitnesses" must have merged these memories together

somehow. Not unexpectedly, many UFO hard-liners responded to "The Roswell Incident: Case Closed" with "Case Reopened." "My analysis," said a member of MUFON (Mutual UFO Network, a scholarly UFO research group), "is that the only dummies there was the U.S. Air Force."[18]

Many UFO enthusiasts rejected the report because they felt it didn't fit with other known facts of the Roswell incident. One oft-raised point is that threats were allegedly made against Roswell locals to keep quiet about what they saw. Consider the following interview that ABC's Charlie Gibson did with UFO researcher Donald Burleson a week following the release of the Air Force's 1997 report:

> *Charles Gibson:* The Air Force did take its opportunity last week to try to lay all the stories to rest, but there are many doubters and nay-sayers, and they seem to have discounted the Air Force report already. Why don't you take a minute, lay out the case. Why are you so sure that they're wrong? Why are you so sure it was some sort of an alien that was visiting from another planet?

> *Donald Burleson:* Well, I think the easy case against the crash dummy cover story is the threats that were made against people. For example, we know that George Wilcox, who was sheriff of Chevas County here in Roswell at the time of the crash, was told that his entire family would be killed if he talked about the debris that he had seen and handled in his office, or if he talked about the retrieval operation that he was seeing under way. And it's a little hard to imagine threats like that over a bunch of silly mannequins, right?

Charles Gibson: Maybe it was some sort of an experimental Air Force program that they don't want people to know about.[19]

Other UFO believers simply took offense at the suggestion that Roswell eyewitnesses were so dumb that they mistook dummies for aliens. "I'm sure I saw those aliens,"[20] said Frank Kaufmann, 80, a retired government intelligence agent. "We were there and know what we saw and there were no dummies there—I know what a dummy looks like. These beings were five-feet-five, small ears, small nose—good-looking."[21]

Because of the strong belief by many people that aliens actually died at Roswell on that fateful day in 1947, a memorial service was held in their honor in conjunction with the Roswell 50th anniversary. About 100 members of the media shadowed 300 others at the service, which included the unveiling of a stone with an inscription that reads: "We don't know who they were, we don't know why they came, we only know they changed our view of the universe."[22]

Abundant Speculations

Why were the alleged aliens here? Speculations abound. A popular theory is that the aliens were here to check out Earth's atomic potential. Three atomic bombs had recently been tested nearby—one just 70 miles away.[23] Concerned about the implications of Earth's atomic capabilities, some aliens showed up to check things out and in the process crashed at Roswell.

A more bizarre speculation surfaced in Showtime's docudrama *Roswell,* which aired in 1994. This docudrama implies that the suicide of James Forrestal—Harry Truman's Secretary of Defense—was caused by his "inability to deal with the enormity of what had been communicated to him telepathically by a captured alien."[24] *Now that's a scary thought.* But where is the proof to back it up? As far as I know, there's not a shred of corroborative evidence to support such a claim.

Some of the most controversial speculations have come from the pen of Philip J. Corso, a retired Army-intelligence officer. In his book *The Day After Roswell*, Corso suggested that government scientists may have taken the wreckage of the alien spacecraft and reverse-engineered alien technology, enabling us to come up with Stealth bombers and incredibly powerful computer systems.[25] The alien wreckage allegedly helped man develop laser technology, fiber optics, night-vision capabilities, and the microchip.[26] Moreover, we read in a *Time* magazine summary of Corso's theory:

> Ever since 1947, when the Roswell crash put the military on alert, the U.S. government has been fighting "the 'real' cold war" against what Corso says the military calls EBEs, or extraterrestrial biological entities. Fortunately, it turns out, Ronald Reagan's Strategic Defense Initiative [SDI] tipped the balance of power. As Corso writes, "[The U.S. and U.S.S.R.] both knew who the real targets of SDI were . . . . When we deployed our advanced particle-beam weapon and tested it in orbit for all to see, the EBEs knew and *we knew* that they knew that we had our defense of the planet in place."[27]

Time magazine, of course, rejected the content of Corso's book. After all, there is no verifiable hard evidence for such claims. However, the *Time* article sparked a letter from the executive producer and cowriter of the 1994 Showtime docudrama *Roswell:*

> As executive producer and cowriter of the 1994 Showtime film *Roswell*, I believe you are wrong to

be dismissive of Philip J. Corso's book *The Day After Roswell*. It is the most important breakthrough on UFOs in a half-century. Here is an author who served as part of President Eisenhower's National Security Council, has 19 medals, and has let the genie out of the bottle on the UFO cover-up. Corso gives the best justification for secrecy about the Roswell Incident ever offered. Those who kept the secret and lied repeatedly to the public to hide the technological manna from heaven end up looking omniscient and justified. He shows how America's interests were served for decades by publicly stone-walling the UFO issue while achieving, in total secrecy, the scientific breakthroughs that literally define our modern world. The debris from the Roswell crash was not manufactured on Earth.[28]

Did Aliens Really Crash at Roswell?

After reading a number of the articles and books that have been published about Roswell, it is hard to say just what happened in this New Mexico city. There is such a preponderance of misinformation, disinformation, distortion of facts, contradicting stories, and seeming exaggerations—all combined with the fact that this happened *over 50 years ago*—that the case for an actual alien crash, in my opinion, simply isn't there. I admit that some of the individual accounts seem to have a certain credibility at first glance, but when one approaches the subject with no leaps of logic, with no speculation, and no subjectivism whatsoever—and instead bases one's view on unbending, sheer objectivism, demanding hard evidence and proof—*the case just isn't there.*

We know that *something* crashed in Roswell, New Mexico; no one disputes that. But when there is a common-sense explanation that coherently ties together the available data, the *greater* burden of proof is on those who hold to the more incredible explanation of an alien spacecraft crashing—and those in that camp simply haven't made an undeniable case for their position.

We need to remember something that Solomon—the wisest man who ever lived (1 Kings 3:12; 4:29-32; 5:12; 10:23)—said on one occasion: "The first to present his case seems right, till another comes forward and questions him" (Proverbs 18:17). Applied to the present issue, the case for an alien crash at Roswell seems to be very strong until further evidence is presented that pokes holes in the theory.

To begin with, many researchers have pointed out that people are giving the government way too much credit in saying it has successfully covered up evidence for a UFO crash all these years. Over the years there have been multiple "leaks" from the White House, revealing sensitive and even incriminating information that the President and other government leaders did not want known. If the government cannot even protect its *own* secrets, what makes anyone think it can keep a UFO landing a secret all these years?

Dean Devlin, cowriter and producer of the movie *Independence Day,* said he was steeped in UFO culture as a boy by a mother who dragged him to UFO conventions. But he doesn't think aliens were involved at Roswell. "I don't know what it was, but our government is so bad at keeping secrets, I have a hard time believing that after all these years the smoking gun hasn't appeared."[29]

The fact of the matter is that the whole Roswell affair involves a confused jumble of anecdotes, rumors, stories, and "eyewitnesses" who actually never saw anything but know someone who knows someone who saw something.[30] And we must be honest with the fact that human memory is not an infallible recording device. Researcher Michael Shermer made the following insightful remarks on human memory as related to the Roswell incident:

> Fifty years is a long time and memories are notoriously unreliable. Does that eyewitness really remember seeing a body in 1947 that looks like an alien, or does he remember 50 years later a crash dummy from 1954 conflated with the memories of books, films, and television shows about aliens? Who can tell at this point? The problem is that memory, however it works, does not work like a video. You cannot rewind, push the play button, and watch your memories unfold. Our memories are constantly edited, deleted, added to, and combined with other memories and experiences. Add an emotional component to the experience and there is no telling what really happened.[31]

It is also a fact that human beings tend to "see" what they're conditioned to see. At the height of the European witch craze that took place in the fifteenth and sixteenth centuries, there were many reports of "flying witches."[32] When spiritualism became big in America and Europe in the nineteenth century, there were many reports of ghosts.[33] "I wouldn't have seen it if I hadn't believed it" seems a fitting twist on an old maxim.[34]

Shermer asks which is more likely—that witches and ghosts and aliens have been and continue to appear to humans, or that humans are experiencing fantasies, misinterpreting natural phenomena, and misremembering experiences in the social context of the age and culture?[35] He concludes:

> I think it can reasonably be argued that such experiences represent a very earthly phenomenon

with a perfectly natural explanation. To me, the fact that humans have such experiences and can be so influenced by culture is at least as fascinating and mysterious as the possibility of aliens landing on Earth. And that is the true meaning of the Roswell Incident.[36]

A note in passing: Though I think Shermer has some good insights on this issue, he is clearly closed to the supernatural as related to the UFO phenomenon. His naturalistic belief system is not open to the possibility of some UFO manifestations being rooted in occultism and demonic phenomena.

We'll be talking about that in a later chapter, so I don't want to dwell on it much here. But I *do* want to remind you what I said earlier in the book: 1) Some UFO sightings are rooted in natural phenomena (which is likely the case with Roswell); 2) Some UFO sightings involve deliberate hoaxes (as is the case with obviously doctored photographs of UFOs); and 3) Some UFO phenomena involve *genuine contact* with entities that I believe are demonic spirits impersonating "alien beings." Cases in this later category invariably involve occultism. (More on all this later.)

Nothing But the Truth?

A closing point that bears mentioning in regard to Roswell is the possibility that some of the "eyewitnesses" at Roswell *have been lying*. Of course, no one likes to point the finger at people and say "liar, liar." But because this issue has captured the popular imagination, a responsible look at Roswell must consider the possibility that some people are quite bluntly lying.

Kal Korff, author of the book *The Roswell UFO Crash: What They Don't Want You to Know*, says there is mounting evidence that many key Roswell witnesses "aren't telling the truth."[37] Korff says that the media are "treating these witnesses with kid gloves."[38]

In a *U.S. News and World Report* article, we read:

> Many of Roswell's key witnesses have changed their stories several times and have been caught telling falsehoods. Korff's book shows that a first group of eyewitnesses mistakenly believed that some debris from a shattered radar reflector came from a spaceship. These witnesses didn't say anything about alien bodies. After a 1989 TV episode of *Unsolved Mysteries* about Roswell, a second melange of "witnesses" came forward with bizarre tales of alien sightings. No one in this second group has told a plausible or consistent story. Jim Ragsdale, for one, said he spotted four alien bodies near a spaceship. Later he asserted that he saw nine alien bodies, from which he removed gold helmets, and that he buried the aliens in the sand.[39]

The *U.S. News and World Report* article also focused some attention on Frank Kaufmann, who has been one of the most oft-quoted "authorities" on the Roswell incident. Kaufmann has been claiming that he was part of a secret military team that recovered the UFO in 1947. However, Kaufmann was discharged from the military in 1945 (two years before the incident). And he has never substantiated his claim that he later worked at the Roswell base in a civilian capacity.[40]

Other researchers have questioned how objective Roswell residents are on the issue of UFOs, especially since UFO tourism brings some $5 million into the city each and every year. Might some people be tempted to, say, "stretch" things a bit if the end result is that more people will visit the city? It makes one wonder!

4

Is There Any Hard Evidence?

If you are making an extraordinary claim, the burden is on you to produce the extraordinary evidence to prove that you are correct; the burden is not on me to prove that you are wrong.

—Astronomer Alan Hale[1]

UFOs are reported to appear seemingly out of nowhere, travel at phenomenal speeds across the sky, turn at impossible angles, and disappear without a trace. In view of this, UFOs are scientifically very hard to explain. One researcher commented that "it is literally impossible to understand them within the space-time framework we use to interpret ordinary events."[2]

UFOs have been sighted virtually around the world. It has been found that no nation is free of UFO reports—and many major nations around the world have officially or secretly engaged in serious investigations of UFOs at the governmental and military level.[3] In fact, in the U.S. alone, tens of millions of dollars have been spent in official UFO investigations by the CIA, FBI, Defense Intelligence Agency, U.S. Air Force, U.S. Army Intelligence, Naval Intelligence, and other organizations.[4]

The truth about UFOs often seems elusive. But those in the UFO community assure us of the reality of extraterrestrials and their spacecrafts. At the end of *The X-Files* credit sequence, we read the words "The truth is out there."[5] We are made to feel that one day contact will occur and irrefutable proof will exist for the UFOs' reality. For now, many people seem willing to take a leap of faith. This point is made succinctly by the pins sold at one UFO museum that simply read BELIEVE.[6]

Skepticism and Cynicism

The scientific community understandably remains skeptical. And the government officially denies the existence or the danger of extraterrestrials and UFOs. The government has, according to its own statements, gone to great lengths to ascertain whether there is any evidence for the existence of extraterrestrials aboard UFOs. In 1948, for example, the U.S. Air Force began the government's first official UFO panel, *Project Sign*, which investigated 243 sightings. It was replaced by *Project Grudge*, which probed another 244 sightings.

In 1952 the most ambitious of the UFO panels, *Project Blue Book*, was set up by the Air Force. Contributing experts for this grand project included physicists, engineers, meteorologists, and an astronomer. *Project Blue Book* had three chief goals: "To explain all reported sightings of UFOs; to decide if UFOs posed a threat to the national security of the United States; and to determine whether UFOs were using any advanced technology that the United States could use."[7]

Then in 1968 the Air Force asked physicist Edward Condon at the University of Colorado to head up a special panel to study the extraterrestrial hypothesis. The panel's report—"A Scientific Study of UFOs," also known as the *Condon Report*[8]— investigated some 59 UFO sightings. The report was reviewed by a special committee of the National Academy of Science and then released in early 1969. The report concluded not only that there was no real evidence of extraterrestrials aboard UFOs, but that any further studies of UFOs should cease.

Based on this report, *Project Blue Book* was closed in December 1969. At the time of its closing, *Project Blue Book* had amassed some 80,000 pages of information on 12,618 reported UFO sightings and events. Each of these sightings was ultimately classified as either "identified" with a known astronomical, atmospheric, or artificial phenomenon (this classification accounted for the great majority of sightings), or as "unidentified," including cases in which information was insufficient.[9]

Many people have responded to government reports by charging there is a conspiracy on the part of the U.S. government—a conspiracy involving the cover-up of alien spacecrafts and the abduction of humans by aliens. It was surprising to me personally to discover that some 50 percent of America's population believes the government is involved in restricting information about extraterrestrials and UFOs. That was the finding in a survey of 1006 adults conducted by Scripps-Howard News Service and Ohio University.[10]

Ted Koppel did a special news program on the Roswell incident, and addressed the problem of charging "cover-up" every time you disagree with someone's findings. Consider his words:

> If I were to dismiss the story [of UFOs] as nothing more than an intriguing but unsubstantiated combination of rumor, misinformation, and legend, I would instantly be regarded as part of the government cover-up, the existence of which is not only assumed but has actually become the most compelling piece of evidence that something did happen. That sort of thing occurs all the time. When

an authority rejects something we fervently believe, we either have to change our belief or we reject the authority.[11]

Though Koppel's words no doubt account for a huge percentage of "cover-up" charges against the U.S. government, there are many UFO enthusiasts who say there is actual *evidence* of a government cover-up. A case in point relates to the alleged crash of a UFO in 1947 in Roswell, which we've discussed previously. Many of the local residents note that the Air Force initially admitted a flying saucer had been found. But then a higher-ranking official stepped in and covered everything up. The government allegedly collected the pieces of the spacecraft and even some alien bodies and threatened locals to remain quiet about everything.

Of course, all this hinges on whom you choose to believe. As I noted in the chapter on Roswell, not only do accounts of Roswell residents contradict each other at points, but some of the "eyewitnesses" have been caught lying. And no one has produced any irrefutable evidence of a massive government cover-up. (I should mention that there *is* a cover-up I'll discuss to which the CIA now admits, but this does not involve a cover-up of UFOs but of spy planes. More on this shortly.)

Another aspect of the cover-up charge relates to the so-called "men in black." The popular movie *Men in Black* pointed to the existence of an alleged secret government agency—the men in black—whose mandate is reportedly to keep the presence of extraterrestrials on Earth a secret from the rest of the planet. Though this movie was a science fiction comedy, the "men in black" legend has been around for some 40 years. The legend involves the claim that there are real men in dark suits whose job it is to use threats, money, and other forms of coercion to keep information about extraterrestrial activity on and around Earth away from the public.[12]

> "I've talked to quite a few people who claim to have had pretty harassing experiences with them," says John Price, who operates the UFO Enigma Museum in Roswell, New Mexico.
>
> Deon Crosby, director of Roswell's International UFO Museum (and Price's competitor), says, "I believe in them. I don't know if they're dressed in black, but I believe wholeheartedly that agents in plain clothes watch everything this museum does and tap our phones."[13]

Such paranoia is dismissed and ridiculed by others. For example, a senior research fellow with the Committee for Scientific Investigation of Claims of the Paranormal (founded by Carl Sagan and Isaac Asimov) says: "There is no evidence that men in black are anything other than hoaxes or urban legends .... It just grows and, every so often, is renewed. These things never go away."[14]

Conspiracy theories and speculations may be interesting, but I now want to move on to one of the most important points of this chapter—that is, *most citings of unidentified flying objects can be easily explained.* Any serious study of the UFO phenomenon must recognize this fundamental point.

Natural Explanations

I will argue in a later chapter that some of the appearances of UFOs in our day—especially those relating to abductions—are actually rooted in occultism and demonic manifestations. But it would be simply incorrect to say that *all* UFO appearances are rooted in occultism.

The fact is that most citings of UFOs are easily explained

in terms of natural phenomena. One researcher recalls a personal experience:

> I was about to give a lecture out at Seattle, Washington . . . around seven o'clock. And before going into the lecture auditorium, several other people were outside. And one of them said, "What's that?" And we looked up, and here was an orange-structured-shape UFO. And I said, "I don't know what it is; maybe it's a balloon reflecting the rays of the setting sun." And the other one said, "No, it's not moving." Somebody said, "Maybe it's a kite." And I said, "Oh, I've never seen a kite that high." It seemed like it was up several thousand feet.
>
> And we stood there, and finally one man said, "I think I've got binoculars in the car." He ran to the car, got his binoculars, looked and said, "It's a kite." Now if that man had not been there, [and] had not had binoculars in the car, I would have to say to you that I had seen an object—in broad daylight—in Seattle, that I could not identify . . . . There are many, many different trigger mechanisms that can generate UFO reports.[15]

This personal experience points to the fact that we must use *discrimination* when evaluating individual UFOs cases. Some UFO appearances will be easily explainable in terms of natural phenomena, while other UFO appearances will in fact be rooted in occultic phenomena. In what immediately follows, my goal is to focus only on those appearances of UFOs that can be explained in terms of natural phenomena.

The reality is that over 90 percent of all reported UFOs prove to be IFOs—that is, *identified flying objects*. Such IFOs can turn out to be the planet Venus, stars, distant airplane landing lights, ball lightning, weather balloons, satellites, formations of birds, lenticular and other strange clouds, windborne objects (such as kites, Frisbees, pieces of paper), blimps or airships, searchlights at night, and various kinds of astronomical and meteorological phenomena. There are all kinds of possibilities.

The ball lightning explanation for UFOs has been explored in some detail by researcher Philip Klass. This little-known kind of lightning, which involves plasma, "is usually oval in shape and an intense red, is often heard to sizzle, and moves around with unpredictable vigor, sometimes hanging motionless, at other times darting about at high speeds with instantaneous changes in direction."[16]

Klass studied some 746 UFO sightings, and in almost every case he discovered that the reported UFOs displayed characteristics typical of plasma—color, shape, erratic movement, and hissing.[17]

> The strong electrical charge of a plasma could also explain the frequent reports of interference with radios, lights, and automobile electrical systems in the vicinity of UFOs. Since a plasma has little mass and is responsive to electromagnetic fields, its erratic flight and high-speed reversals of direction posed no theoretical problem. Moreover, plasmas reflect radio waves, so they cannot be ruled out when UFOs appear on radar screens.[18]

Klass's theory certainly explains at least some of the reported sightings of UFOs. He wrote that ball lightning may "explain many sightings of lower-altitude 'unidentified flying objects.'"[19]

Dr. Hugh Ross, president of Reasons to Believe (a Christian ministry), believes that probably half of the UFO sightings reported are actually the planet Venus, which often appears to be a very bright morning star and can even appear during the daytime hours.[20] Ross also notes that on occasion birds that have been exposed to phosphorous (glowing) dust and migrate during the nighttime hours have sometimes been mistaken for UFOs.[21]

Further Explanations

There are still further possible explanations for UFO sightings. For example, we now know that the military is working on various methods of displaying 3-D (three-dimensional) holographic images in the sky as a form of nonlethal weaponry. Obviously such images would not be detected by radar, which is consistent with many UFO reports.[22] Someone could easily see such an image in the sky and think it was an alien spacecraft.

There are also various "black projects" or secret projects that the government has been engaged in. In the late 1950s and early 1960s one of these projects involved a saucer-shaped craft that could hover above the ground. This craft no doubt accounts for some of the UFO sightings that occurred in the Washington State area during that time frame.[23]

In 1997 there was a deluge of UFO sightings one night in Arizona. In fact, some strange lights were captured on videotape. In this case it turns out that visiting jets from the Maryland Air National Guard were using high-intensity flares over a bombing range near Phoenix that night.[24]

> The planes were dropping high-intensity flares from 15,000 feet to illuminate the target area . . . . The flares fall slowly by parachute and illuminate a wide area. Before returning to Davis-Monthan Air Force Base in Tucson that night, the planes dumped all their remaining flares at high altitude,

which would have created what one pilot called "one hell of a light show."[25]

A key factor to keep in mind regarding all this is that according to many experts, the human eye can easily be tricked, even to the point of hallucination:

A bright light, such as the planet Venus, often appears to move, though a clamped telescope or a sighting bar shows it to be fixed. A visual impression of distance is also unreliable because it is based on an assumed size. Reflections from windows or eyeglasses may provide superimposed views. Optical defects can turn point sources of light into apparently saucer-shaped objects. Such optical illusions coupled with a *desire* to interpret visual images account for many UFO reports.[26]

Moreover, experts have pointed out how much junk is floating around in outer space, so there are plenty of opportunities for the human eye to be tricked:

There are 7087 man-made objects in space. They include ten screws, each an eighth of an inch in diameter, that were discarded during a 1984 shuttle mission; a thermal glove that floated out of Gemini 4 in 1965; a screwdriver dropped by a careless space-walking cosmonaut aboard the Soviet Mir space station; and several thousand satellites, some actively communicating with ground stations, and some relics, useless twentieth-century antiques that will continue to whiz and clank through space for generations. All this hectic traffic above the planet Earth is constantly monitored by the U.S. Space Command's Space Surveillance Center hidden inside snowcapped Cheyenne Mountain near Colorado Springs.[27]

All of this means that when one sees a UFO, one is on safest ground assuming that there is a natural explanation. Now it could be that there is not a natural explanation—and in that case it may involve occultism or demonic phenomena. But a good starting point is to suspect a natural explanation. The 1969 final report of "Project Colorado," set up at the University of Colorado and independent of the Air Force, states in part:

> The report recognizes that there remain UFO sightings that are not easily explained. The report does suggest, however, so many reasonable and possible directions in which an explanation may eventually be found that there seems to be no reason to attribute them to an extraterrestrial source without evidence that is much more convincing . . . . On the basis of present knowledge, the least likely explanation of UFOs is the hypothesis of extraterrestrial visitations by intelligent beings.[28]

My point, then, is that many reported UFOs actually turn out to be IFOs—identified flying objects. Again, for those objects that remain truly unidentifiable, it may be that occultism is involved. Occultism is particularly to be suspected in cases were alleged "alien abduction" has occurred.

A Brief Interview with Philip Klass

Because Philip Klass has apparently made it his life's purpose to force UFO advocates to come up with hard evidence to support their views, please indulge me if I cite his responses a bit more than anyone else in this chapter. Klass granted a brief interview to Nova Online (an Internet site), and he was asked how compelling he thought the evidence was for the existence of UFOs. Though his answer deals primarily with abduction claims, he demonstrates quite forcefully just how *uncompelling* much of the physical evidence is:

> The evidence, first off, is not universal and it is not compelling. Budd Hopkins likes to claim that anyone with a scar on their body, [and] they cannot remember how they got it . . . that that scar was caused by aliens. Nonsense.
>
> When I give UFO lectures, I ask people in the audience: "How many of you have a scar on your body somewhere?" And nearly every hand goes up. And then when I ask, "Can you remember how you got the scar?" almost no hands go up. Because most of our scars and bodily injuries— particularly the minor ones—occur when we're children, when we are learning how to roller-skate and ride bicycles and doing the sort of things where we injure ourselves.
>
> Missing time is supposed to be another mark of abduction. Heavens, I experience missing time every time I look at my watch and say: "My goodness, it's two p.m., I thought it was only around noon." When I go for a drive, I typically experience missing time, because I don't recall passing this bridge or passing that bridge. It is automatic. It is routine.
>
> . . . So—now it is claimed that the aliens leave implants [up peoples' noses, for example] . . . . Now, wait a minute. If aliens are abducting thousands or millions of Americans, and if they're

putting implants in many of them, all it would take would be one little micro electronic, or one unusual device that we could say: "This could not have been made on this earth." And that would be the evidence that would convince even me. But so far, they cannot come up with any scientifically credible evidence.[29]

The Need for *Irrefutable* Proof

If it were true that extraterrestrials were visiting this planet in spacecraft that seem to defy the laws of physics, this would unquestionably rank as the greatest discovery in the history of science. That being the case, in order for people to accept it and believe it, there must be extraordinary evidence to prove it.

As astronomer Alan Hale put it, "If you are making an extraordinary claim, the burden is on you to produce the extraordinary evidence to prove that you are correct; the burden is not on me to prove that you are wrong." Furthermore, Hale argues, "you must prove your case by providing the direct and compelling evidence for it; you can't prove it by eliminating a few token explanations and then crying, 'Well, what else can it be?'"[30]

It makes good sense that if one is confronted with a series of phenomena for which there exists more than one viable explanation, one should choose the simplest explanation that fits all the available data. It is true that many people have seen things in the sky for which they have no explanation. But it is also true, as Hale notes, that "reports can come from people who are unaware of the various phenomena that are visible in the sky and from people who are not equipped or trained at making reliable scientific observations."[31] That's why people shouldn't make dogmatic claims about UFOs when the evidence is so flimsy.

New Light from the CIA

A recent admission by the CIA (Central Intelligence Agency) further confirms that many UFO reports are rooted in natural phenomena. In 1997 the CIA admitted in a study that the Air Force lied to the public about UFO sightings in the 1950s and 1960s. Gerald K. Haines, a historian at the National Reconnaissance Office, wrote in the 1997 study that during the Cold War years, the Air Force frequently provided explanations for UFO sightings that were untrue in order to deflect attention away from the supersecret spy planes they were using. "Over half of all UFO reports from the late 1950s through the 1960s were accounted for by manned reconnaissance flights (namely the U-2) over the United States," Haines said.[32]

These early spy planes—called "U-2s"—were silver and reflected the sun's rays, especially at sunrise and sunset. They often appeared as fiery objects to people at the ground level. Because of this the U-2s were later painted black.[33]

Haines noted that concern about the public finding out about the secret spy planes "led the Air Force to make misleading and deceptive statements to the public in order to allay public fears and to protect an extraordinarily sensitive national security project."[34] During these years U.S. officials were fearful that the Soviets would attempt to disrupt America's air defense system or the government itself by orchestrating mass UFO sightings.

It was this concern that prompted Air Force officials to play down the UFO issue and concoct false stories to explain away sightings of alleged "flying saucers." In this sense, then, there was a "cover-up." But the whole goal was to deflect attention away from America's supersecret spy planes that were considered crucial to national security.[35]

Haines said a special panel studying the issue concluded that "potential enemies contemplating an attack on the United

States might exploit the UFO phenomena and use them to disrupt U.S. air defenses."[36] Moreover, the panel found "that continued emphasis on UFO reporting might threaten the orderly functioning of the government by clogging the channels of communication with irrelevant reports and by inducing hysterical mass behavior harmful to constituted authority."[37]

Haines concedes that "while perhaps justified, this deception added fuel to the later conspiracy theories and the cover-up controversy."[38]

All of this is simply to say that many of the UFO reports that took place in the 1950s and 1960s were actually U.S. spy planes. People can debate over whether the government should have lied. But the lying aside, the point I am making is that these planes constitute a natural explanation for a great many sightings. This adds further support to my earlier statement that unless there is good reason to believe otherwise (such as occultic phenomena), one's *first best assumption* should be that the sighting is rooted in natural phenomena.

5

Are UFOs Mentioned in the Bible?

UFOs could well be part of the same larger intelligence which has shaped the tapestry of religion and mythology since the dawn of human consciousness.
—J. Allen Hynek[1]

> *On the morning of the third day there was thunder and lightning, with a thick cloud over the mountain, and a very loud trumpet blast. Everyone in the camp trembled. Then Moses led the people out of the camp to meet with God, and they stood at the foot of the mountain. Mount Sinai was covered with smoke, because the LORD descended on it in fire. The smoke billowed up from it like smoke from a furnace, the whole mountain trembled violently, and the sound of the trumpet grew louder and louder. Then Moses spoke and the voice of God answered him. The LORD descended to the top of Mount Sinai and called Moses to the top of the mountain. So Moses went up . . . .*
—Moses in Exodus 19:16-20

D id Moses and the people of Israel have an awe-inspiring encounter with an extraterrestrial on Mount Sinai? Was this magnificent alien so resplendently glorious and powerful that the Israelites mistook it for being God? Do the mentions of thick smoke, fire, and loud sounds indicate that a starship actually landed on the mountain? To listen to many people today, one would think so.

In fact, in recent times numerous elaborate arguments for UFOs in the Bible have been concocted by various people. Many of the more notable arguments are found in Erich Von Daniken's controversial book *Chariots of the Gods,* which has sold more than 45 million copies since its release in the late 1960s.[2] Von Daniken argued that the ark of the covenant was actually a radio transmitter that enabled Moses to communicate with beings in a spaceship that guided the Israelites across the wilderness during the Exodus.

According to Von Doniken, the Bible, for lack of better terms (the ancients were limited in their knowledge), calls these spacecrafts "pillar of fire" by night and a "pillar of cloud" by day (Exodus 13:21,22; 14:19,20).[3] (This reminds me of the movie *Independence Day,* for whenever alien spacecrafts showed up in Earth's atmosphere, they were accompanied by clouds and fire.)[4]

It has been suggested by a Presbyterian minister, who is quite open to the possibility of UFOs in the Bible, that the parting of the Red Sea was actually brought about by the exhaust of UFO spacecrafts. Moses needed help because the Egyptians were pursuing them. So Moses quickly contacted the aliens with his radio transmitter (the ark of the covenant), and the aliens blew open a path through the Red Sea by the exhaust of the ship.[5]

More than one UFO enthusiast has suggested that Moses did not encounter God Almighty in the burning bush; rather, he came into contact with an exalted alien whose appearance was awesome. Erich Von Daniken even wrote a book entitled *Was God an Astronaut?* in which he argued that the various religions of humankind arose from alien contact.[6] This, of course, effectively robs Christianity of everything miraculous.

> God, the transcendent Creator and miracle-worker of Judeo-Christian thought, becomes a technician and scientist whose knowledge and skill by far surpass those of human beings. God's activities do not require supernatural explanations, for they are nothing but practical and medical procedures that are so advanced that they appear miraculous or magical in the context of our inferior and underdeveloped culture.[7]

Did Ezekiel Encounter a UFO?

Perhaps the most famous allegation of extraterrestrial contact in the Bible relates to Ezekiel 1. Consider these words:

> I looked, and I saw a windstorm coming out of the north—an immense cloud with flashing lightning and surrounded by brilliant light. The center of the fire looked like glowing metal, and in the fire was what looked like four living creatures. In appearance their form was that of a man, but each of them had four faces and four wings . . . .
>
> As I looked at the living creatures, I saw a wheel on the ground beside each creature with its four faces. This was the appearance and structure of the wheels: They sparkled like chrysolite, and all four looked alike. Each appeared to be made like a wheel intersecting a wheel. As they moved, they would go in any one of the four directions the

creatures faced; the wheels did not turn about as the creatures went. Their rims were high and awesome, and all four rims were full of eyes all around (Ezekiel 1:4,6,15,18).

Von Daniken and other UFO enthusiasts have suggested that the Old Testament prophet Ezekiel saw a flying saucer. Ezekiel first beheld a windstorm out of the north. (Keep in mind that in *Independence Day* and in Steven Spielberg's *Close Encounters of the Third Kind*, appearances of UFO spacecraft always involved atmospheric disturbances.) Then Ezekiel saw wheels (perhaps rotating rims with lights) that gave the appearance of having eyes all around the rim. There were resplendently beautiful aliens in the midst of these starships.

While most scholars scoffed at Von Daniken's suggestion, an engineer with the National Aeronautics and Space Administration soon became a believer. Josef F. Blumrich was initially skeptical, like all other scholars. However, knowing something about spacecraft design, he determined that what Ezekiel described might in fact be a feasible design for landing modules from a mothership.

Blumrich worked out the design in some detail and then published the results in a 1973 book entitled *The Spaceships of Ezekiel*. He concluded that the four "living creatures" may have been four sets of landing gear, each one with a "wheel" for maneuvering over the ground. The "wings" of each craft, he said, were probably similar to helicopter blades that were used for precision positioning prior to touchdown. A rocket engine on each craft explains the presence of fire.[8]

Otherworldly Explanations for Jesus Christ

Of great fascination is the fact that Jesus Christ has been related to appearances of UFOs in the Bible. We begin with the virgin birth. Of course, the orthodox Christian view is that the

Holy Spirit overshadowed Mary, thereby causing Mary to become pregnant (Luke 1:35). The eternal Son of God stepped out of eternity and into humanity in Mary's womb.

Quite different is the explanation of some UFO enthusiasts. Some believe that aliens aboard a spacecraft injected Mary with the sperm of a space creature from another world. Others claim that the angel Gabriel of the Gospels was actually an alien scientist who artificially inseminated the Virgin Mary to create Jesus.[9] In such a scenario, of course, Mary can still obviously be called a virgin because she had not had sexual relations with anyone. But there was no miracle, as orthodox Christianity has claimed since the first century.[10] Jesus was in reality a mixed breed—part human and part alien. This accounts for His seemingly supernatural powers.

Soon after the birth of Christ, aliens appeared to shepherds in a field to announce this astonishing event.[11] It is understandable that the shepherds mistook these aliens for angels, but it was really aliens who informed the shepherds of the news.

Aliens were involved in other ways in the life of Christ. For example, it wasn't really a "star of Bethlehem" that led the Magi to the home of Jesus (Matthew 2:7). It was rather a spacecraft flying high in the atmosphere, leading the Magi just as spacecrafts had earlier led the Israelites in the wilderness as a "pillar of fire."[12]

And during Jesus' baptism, the Spirit did not descend upon Jesus in the form of a dove (Matthew 3). Rather, there was some kind of energy discharge from a spacecraft hovering in the sky that came upon Jesus.[13]

Did Jesus really perform miracles among His people, as the New Testament indicates? No, we are told. Aliens aboard UFOs were involved in all the works Jesus did on earth:

> The Gospels relate many stories about how Jesus
> cured the crippled and the lame . . . . These were

not genuine miraculous cures . . . . What actually took place was that extraterrestrials had previously hypnotized certain people so that their infirmities were psychosomatic. These apparently sick people were programmed to respond to the suggestions of Jesus that led to their being instantaneously healed.[14]

Sometime later, Moses and Elijah appeared to Jesus at the Mount of Transfiguration. UFO enthusiasts tell us that the mention of a "bright cloud" (Matthew 17:5) indicates that it was actually a spacecraft that served to transport Moses and Elijah to this mountain from a higher level of reality.[15] After their conversation with Jesus was over, they boarded the spacecraft and left the mountain.

When Jesus ascended into heaven, this also allegedly involved a spacecraft. The biblical text says, "After he said this, he was taken up before their very eyes, and a cloud hid him from their sight" (Acts 1:9). The means of being "taken up" was an alien ship of some type[16]—and, as is the case with other appearances of spacecrafts, clouds were present.

Some go so far as to say that Jesus was a participant in a grand experiment on humanity:

What if it turns out that the aliens are really the gods of the Bible? That is, the all-powerful beings who have been here before, done their thing, left, and now come back to throw their technological hat into the ring? Suppose they had been here two thousand years ago and had subsequently traveled at almost the speed of light so that time slowed down for them while it went on for the people they left behind? They might be the same beings who were here in Jesus' time, and had left Jesus or other religious leaders behind and are now back to check on how things had gone.

That sounds like science fiction, but when you recognize that Einsteinian relativity indicates that for people traveling at extremely high speed time slows down, then we have the startling possibility that we are an old experiment being evaluated. They may not be terribly impressed by the ways we've learned to kill each other, or our inability to meet many of the basic needs of so many people on our planet.[17]

UFOs, Angels, and Theology

Still another way that UFOs have been interpreted to be within the pages of Holy Writ relates to the transportation of angels. Barry H. Downing, a clergyman, argues that UFOs are part of a "heavenly transportation system" carrying angels of God who interact with man. This is not something that can actually be proven, Downing concedes, but is something that must be accepted by faith.[18]

Downing believes that UFOs come from a parallel universe—"in the midst of us"—citing a statement by Jesus (Luke 17:21). The modern UFO mystery, in his view, is merely an extension of events depicted in the Bible and other historical reports showing that angels "are still with us, doing their shepherd work—by night and day."[19]

Some UFOlogists have claimed that some of the content of the Bible was actually brought to this planet by aliens. The doctrine of hell is an example:

Dr. Irwin Ginsburgh, a leading physicist, suggests that the biblical description of hell could well be a description of the Planet Venus, and a description transplanted to Planet Earth by space beings. It has been discovered that Venus has a seering atmosphere, with a surface heat of 850 degrees Fahrenheit. The planet is wreathed in dense sulfur clouds, with sulfuric acid droplets—liquid and solid, dripping from the clouds. Could our planetary neighbor be the origin of our hell? Dr. Ginsburgh thinks it could be.

It could be that knowledge of the surface conditions on Venus were communicated to primitive Earth people by extraterrestrials who showed them pictures of the planet's surface . . . and the dark, glowing, searing hot and sulfurous planet has been remembered—as hell.[20]

A thought in passing: In the next chapter, "The New Age Embrace of UFOs," I will point out that some UFO cults believe Venus to be a "spiritual planet" where Cosmic Masters (including Jesus) now live. Somehow Dr. Ginsburgh's description of Venus doesn't fit the utopian New Age description of Venus.

It should now be obvious to the reader that many UFOlogists explain the emergence of religion on planet Earth as entirely the result of UFO activity among human beings in the past. It is speculated that in ancient times extraterrestrials might have been interpreted to be angels, gods, or God. We are told that the gods of mythology were in reality extraterrestrial astronauts.[21]

"Whatever the visitors are," abductee Whitley Strieber writes in *Transformation,* his 1988 sequel to *Communion,* "I suspect they have been responsible for much paranormal phenomena, ranging from the appearance of gods, angels, fairies, ghosts, and miraculous beings to the landing of UFOs in the backyards of America." If this is the case, then, in Strieber's words, "we may very well be something different from what we believe ourselves to be, on this earth for reasons that may not yet be known to us, the understanding of which will be an immense challenge."[22]

Are UFOs *Really* in the Bible?

I do not believe for a minute that UFOs are in the Bible. In every case mentioned previously, UFOlogists are reading their own meanings *into* the biblical text (eisogesis) rather than drawing their meanings *from* the biblical text (exegesis).

Allow me to illustrate. By using eisogesis instead of exegesis, a Marxist interpreter could so skew the meaning of the U.S. Constitution that it came out reading like a communistic document. UFOlogists have done this same type of thing with the Bible. They so skew the meaning of the biblical text that it comes out saying something entirely different from what was intended by the biblical author.

Instead of superimposing a meaning *onto* the biblical text, the objective interpreter seeks to discover the author's intended meaning (the only *true* meaning). One must recognize that what a passage means is fixed by the author and is not subject to alteration by readers. Meaning is *determined* by the author; it is *discovered* by readers. And a singular key to determining the intended meaning of the author is reading the verse *in context*. With this in mind, let's look at some of the claims made by UFO enthusiasts.

1. *Pillars of fire.* Exodus 13 and 14 indicate that during the Israelites' Exodus sojourn, "the Lord" was with them in a very visible and reassuring way. He went ahead of them in a pillar of cloud *by day* and in a pillar of fire *by night*. This way they could travel either by day *or* by night (Exodus 13:21). We are specifically told in Exodus 14:19 that the "angel of God" was behind these phenomena (not UFOs). The angel of God was a manifestation of God Himself (Exodus 3:14), and whenever He

moved in front of or in back of the Israelites, the cloud and fire moved with Him. There is no presence of a spacecraft anywhere in the context.

2. *Ark of the covenant.* It is nonsense to suggest that the ark of the covenant was a radio transmitter. Scripture provides us concise details about the ark and its function. The specifications for the ark are provided in Exodus 25:10-22. Scripture indicates that the ark symbolized God's presence (1 Samuel 4:3-22). It served as the container of the covenant stones, which were a continual reminder of the covenant between God and Israel (Exodus 25:16, 21). It also contained the pot of manna, which symbolized the bread of God from heaven (Exodus 16:33). Aaron's rod was later placed in it as a witness to Israel of God's choice of the priesthood (Numbers 17:10).

3. *Parting of the Red Sea.* As the Egyptians were moving in to attack the Israelites, Moses spoke some of his most famous words: "Do not be afraid. Stand firm and you will see the deliverance the LORD will bring you today" (Exodus 14:13). Indeed, said Moses, "the LORD will fight for you; you need only to be still" (verse 14). (Notice that "the LORD" does these things, not UFOs.)

The Lord then told Moses to take a step of faith and walk toward the Red Sea (Exodus 14:15). As the people moved toward the sea, Moses was told by God to raise his staff—the *same* staff that had been used by God to inflict many miraculous plagues on Egypt (verses 16-18).

As Moses stretched out his hand—indicating to all present that what was about to happen was not a natural phenomenon—*the* LORD (not a UFO) split the sea by a strong east wind (Exodus 14:21). This was no shallow body of water. We are not told precisely how deep the water was, but it was deep enough that the Egyptian army drowned when God brought the waters back together again (verse 28). Moreover, we are not speaking of a narrow dividing of water. Again, we don't know precisely how wide it was, but it had to be sufficient for over 2 million Israelites to pass through to the other side along with their flocks and herds.

Such a miracle—with that great a volume of water displaced for that length of time—required far more power than an alien spacecraft would have in its tailpipe. This required the very power of God.

4. *Mount Sinai.* Exodus 19:16-20 is a description not of a spacecraft landing on Mount Sinai but of God Himself coming down on the mountain. According to instructions given to Moses, on the third day the Lord would come down onto Mount Sinai (Exodus 19:11). This was in contrast to pagan deities, who supposedly *dwelt* on the mountains. (For example, Greek gods were believed to live on Mount Olympus.) Scripture depicts God as dwelling *in heaven* (1 Kings 8:30-49; John 8:23); hence, He would have to "come down" in order to meet the people on the mountain. As promised, on the third day God descended to Mount Sinai and gave an awesome display of His power and majesty (Exodus 19:16-19). There was thunder, lightning, a thick cloud, and a very loud trumpet blast. Alien UFOs are nowhere in the context.

5. *UFOs in Ezekiel.* Using exegesis instead of eisogesis, it becomes clear that Ezekiel did not encounter a UFO but rather experienced a vision of the glory of God. This is evident for several reasons. First, the text states clearly that "this was the appearance of the likeness of the glory of the Lord" (Ezekiel 1:28). Moreover, it is called "visions" in the very first verse. Visions are usually couched in highly symbolic form (see Revelation 1:9-20). Hence, the "likeness" (verse 28) given of things should not be taken literally but symbolically.

It is also clear from the context that the "living creatures" were angels because they had "wings" (Ezekiel 1:6) and flew in the midst of heaven (see Ezekiel 10). They compare to the angels mentioned in Isaiah 6:2 and especially the "living creatures" (angels) that are described as being around God's throne (Revelation 4:6).

The message from these beings was from the "Sovereign LORD" of Israel to the prophet Ezekiel (Ezekiel 2:1-4), not one from some alleged UFO aliens. The context was a message from the God of Israel through the Jewish prophet Ezekiel to His "rebellious nation" (2:3,4; see 3:4). Contextually, the UFO interpretation is impossible.

6. *The virgin birth.* The virgin birth was not the result of alien activity but rather was primarily the work of the Holy Spirit. The Spirit's ministry was necessary because of Christ's deity and preexistence (see Isaiah 7:14; 9:6; Galatians 4:4). The Holy Spirit's supernatural work in Mary's body enabled Christ—as eternal God—to take on a human nature. And through this incarnation, a key component of the plan of salvation that was conceived in eternity past came to fruition. Our eternal Savior became flesh with the specific purpose of dying on our behalf so that those who trusted in Him could become saved and dwell with God forever (John 3:16,17).

Through the miracle of the virgin birth, the eternal Son of the eternal God reached out and took to Himself a true and complete humanity without diminishing His essential deity. He united deity and humanity inseparably and eternally in one Person.

Though the Holy Spirit played the central role in the incarnation and was the agent through whom the incarnation was brought about (Luke 1:35), we are told in Hebrews 10:5 that it was *the Father* who prepared a human body for Christ. Moreover, *Jesus* is said to have taken upon Himself flesh and blood—as if it were an act of His own individual will (Hebrews 2:14). Therefore, all three persons of the Trinity were sovereignly involved in Jesus' taking on human flesh in the incarnation. Alien beings were nowhere in sight.

7. *The angel Gabriel*. The name "Gabriel" literally means "mighty one of God." The name speaks of Gabriel's incredible power as endowed by God. He is distinguished as *an angel* (not an alien scientist) that stands in the very presence of God (Luke 1:19), evidently in some preeminent sense. His high rank in the angelic realm is obvious from both his name and his continuous standing in the presence of God.

Gabriel is portrayed in Scripture as one who brings revelation to the people of God regarding God's purpose and program. For example, in the Old Testament Gabriel revealed the future by interpreting a vision for Daniel (8:17), and gave understanding and wisdom to him (9:22). In the New Testament (some 500 years later), Gabriel brought the message to Zacharias about the birth of John the Baptist, and announced the birth of Jesus to the Virgin Mary (Luke 1:18,19,26-38). (Note that Gabriel announced—*not caused*—the birth of Jesus.)

8. *Jesus' miracles*. Jesus' miracles were not healings of psychosomatically induced illnesses arranged by aliens. Rather, His miracles were bona fide supernatural events brought about by His divine power as the Messiah.

Note that John's Gospel always refers to the miracles of Jesus as "signs." This word emphasizes the *significance* of the action rather than the marvel (John 4:54; 6:14; 9:16). These signs were strategically performed by Jesus to *signify* His true identity and glory.

In the process of proving His identity, Jesus demonstrated His control of nature (such as calming a storm—Matthew 8:23-27), He healed many people of bodily afflictions (such as an invalid—John 5:1-15), and He raised people from the dead (such as Lazarus—John 11). One wonders how Lazarus could be said to have been psychosomatically dead, with his body stinking from the decay of death for several days. One also wonders how Jesus' control of the weather and turning water into wine were psychosomatic phenomena.

9. *Jesus' ascension.* Acts 1:9 tells us, "After he said this, he was taken up before their very eyes, and a cloud hid him from their sight." The verse says nothing about a spacecraft. That is reading something into the text that is simply not there. The words "taken up" simply indicate that Christ visibly and physically ascended in bodily fashion *straight up* and *into heaven.* The presence of clouds are likely a reference to the visible glory of God, as is the case elsewhere in Scripture (see Matthew 17:5; 24:30; 26:64). Christ was engulfed in the glory of God as He vanished from the sight of the disciples.

10. *Angels in UFOs.* Angels do not need spacecraft in order to travel, but rather have been specially endowed by God with a capacity to fly. We read of the angels surrounding God's throne that they have six wings: "With two wings they covered their faces, with two they covered their feet, and *with two they were flying*" (Isaiah 6:2, emphasis added). The angel Gabriel apparently has the ability to fly swiftly—perhaps faster than most of the other angels (Daniel 9:21). In Revelation 14:6 an angel is portrayed as flying through the air in earth's atmosphere. Angels have no need for vehicular assistance.

11. *Hell as the planet Venus.* "Hell" is not the planet Venus. The Scriptures assure us that hell is a real place *specially created by God* to accommodate the banishment of Satan and his fallen angels who rebelled against God. Human beings who reject Christ will join Satan and his fallen angels in this infernal place of suffering (see Matthew 25:41).

I should note that some scholars believe the "fire" of hell is quite literal while others believe "fire" is a metaphorical way of expressing the great wrath of God. Scripture tells us: "The Lord your God is a consuming fire, a jealous God" (Deuteronomy 4:24). "God is a consuming fire" (Hebrews 12:29). "His wrath is poured out like fire" (Nahum 1:6). "Who can stand when he appears? For he will be like a refiner's fire . . . " (Malachi 3:2). God said, "My wrath will break out and burn like fire because of the evil you have done—burn with no one to quench it" (Jeremiah 4:4). Whether the fire of hell is literal or metaphorical, it will entail horrible suffering for those who are there.

In view of this brief summary, it is more than clear that UFO enthusiasts are simply reading their fanciful and bizarre ideas into Scripture rather than drawing the true meaning out of Scripture. There is not a single verse in Scripture, taken in context, that gives even the slightest support for UFO phenomena.

Here is something for you to think about, however. If you were Satan, and were using demonic spirits to impersonate aliens, communicate New Age doctrines (see Chapters 6 and 7) and draw people into occultism (see Chapter 8), would it not make a good strategy on the part of the powers of darkness to promote the idea that UFOs are in the Bible? What better way to give credence to UFOs than to apparently show their presence within the pages of Holy Writ?

Christians beware! Deceptive spirits are at work!

6

The New Age Embrace of UFOs

In the last 30 years the extraterrestrials have been accelerating their interaction with us in preparation for a fast-approaching time of transition and transformation.

—Brad Steiger[1]

Shirley MacLaine, according to her testimony in the book *Out On a Limb*, was introduced to the idea of extraterrestrials and UFOs by her spiritual mentor David.[2] David had had contact (allegedly) with an extraterrestrial named "the Mayan." While David and Shirley were on a trip to Peru (a spiritual pilgrimage of sorts), she had an opportunity to meditate. During her meditation, she claims, a UFO flew over her head and "I began to have flashing feelings coming toward me in another language."[3] MacLaine now says the book *Out On a Limb* was indirectly inspired by the Mayan.[4] She also says she has been chosen by extraterrestrials to spread the word regarding the coming New Age.[5] (The "New Age" is often defined as a time of enlightenment and harmony characterized by oneness with God ["all is God"] and the brotherhood of man.)

Antonio Huneeus, a reporter sympathetic to MacLaine, comments that "an important part of Shirley MacLaine's message has to do with her conviction that we are not alone, and that extraterrestrial civilizations have visited Earth in the past, and continue to do so at an increasing pace." Indeed, Huneeus says, "this realization came to her during a gradual process of becoming acquainted—and accepting—other non-mainstream ideas like reincarnation, spiritualism and channeling, eastern meditation, etc., which led to her experience of a divine cosmic energy, or God-force, which she says exists within all of us."[6]

One can detect in MacLaine's New Age spiritual pilgrimage the clear connection between occultism and UFOs. (The word "occult" comes from the Latin *occultus*, meaning "secret" or "hidden." The word is often used in contexts of seeking secret knowledge by methods forbidden by God, such as spiritism. We will deal with occultism in detail in Chapters 8 and 9.) It is sobering to realize that MacLaine—with her emphasis on UFOs—is representative of virtually millions of New Agers around the world. As we will see in the following, belief in UFOs is at the very heart of New Age theology.

The Alien Agenda in the New Age

An examination of the evidence indicates beyond any doubt that a primary agenda of the alien "visitors"—*whoever* or *whatever* they are—is to change the way human beings think about God and His Word (the Bible), and to replace exclusivistic Christianity with a religion of universalism.[7] As well, the visitors seem intent on drawing people deeper and deeper into various forms of occultism—including divination, out-of-body experiences, levitation, clairvoyance, and spiritism. (Don't be concerned if you're unfamiliar with these terms; they will be defined in Chapter 8, which deals specifically with occultism.)

Jacques Vallee, a longtime researcher of UFO phenomena (and the real-life model for the French scientist in Steven

Spielberg's *Close Encounters of the Third Kind*), suggests that the "visitors" are purposely hoping to change our belief systems and are engaging in a "worldwide enterprise of 'subliminal seduction.'"[8] In his book *The Invisible College*, Vallee argues that "human belief . . . is being controlled and conditioned." Indeed, "man's concepts are being rearranged," and we may be headed toward "a massive change of human attitudes toward paranormal abilities and extraterrestrial life."[9] ("Paranormal" refers to phenomena *beyond* the normal.)

Vallee notes that the methods of the "aliens" are those of deception: "systematic manipulation of witnesses and contactees; covert use of various sects and cults; and control of the channels through which alleged 'space messages' can make an impact on the public."[10] By using such deception, these alien entities are attempting to change the way humans think.

Vallee is not alone in this opinion. Whitley Strieber, bestselling author who claims to have been abducted by aliens (which he documents in his book *Communion*), acknowledges that the visitors are attempting to affect the way humans think. He says they seem to be "orchestrating our awareness of them very carefully," and seem to be seeking "a degree of influence or even control over us."[11] Strieber admitted that the visitors "have caused me to slough off my old view of the world like the dismal skin that it was and seek a completely new vision of this magnificent, mysterious, and fiercely alive universe."[12]

My friend John Weldon, a Christian researcher who has been investigating the UFO phenomenon for many years, says the visitors seek "to deliberately move significant portions of an entire culture, or world, into acceptance of or involvement in the occult, and a collective alteration in worldview. This is preparatory for and necessary to the events surrounding the rise of the Antichrist [the final anti-God world leader who will come into control of the world in the end times]."[13] Weldon, who believes the "aliens" are really demonic spirits, says they "are here to misguide the multitudes and they are doing pretty well. [The 'aliens'] have judiciously utilized their powers through selected people to fascinate the masses, and they have widely promulgated their doctrines."[14]

I think Weldon's point is extremely important. Indeed, it seems that occultism has now penetrated the mainstream of American culture. We can even call a 900-number and for $3.95 per minute talk to a "certified" psychic who can give us guidance on all of life's problems. This occultic worldview that has gained such a foothold in this country may very well be laying the groundwork for the future occultic works of the Antichrist during the tribulation period (see 2 Thessalonians 2:9).

A discerning pastor I read about commented:

> It may be that UFOs are reeducating mankind to accept a casual familiarity with paranormal activity . . . . From Satan's standpoint, UFOs may be preparing the modern mind to accept a casual familiarity with supernatural phenomena. This would facilitate the Antichrist's reign, and until then, create a milieu in which evil spirits may operate more freely.[15]

The Alien Message

I have noticed a pattern: Whereas the actions and messages of the "aliens" are consistently *occultic* in nature, they are also *anti-Christian* in nature. They never say things that affirm the Bible as God's Word. They never say anything that even remotely glorifies Christ. They never say anything about man's sin problem or his need for redemption. They never say anything about Christ's redemptive work at the cross.

90

Instead, the "aliens" talk about attaining cosmic awareness and transcendence to a higher spiritual plane. They consistently encourage participation in a variety of occultic practices—including astral projection, automatic handwriting, channeling (spiritism), levitation, and clairvoyance. Everything they say and do betrays their true identity. These "aliens" or "space brothers" are, I believe, actually *demons against God* (more on this in Chapter 11). The point I want to make at this juncture is simply that the alien agenda among human beings is in fact a *demonic* agenda.

The Urantia Book: The Alien Agenda Illustrated

I will illustrate the demonic agenda of the "aliens" in many ways throughout the rest of this book. A preliminary illustration may be found in those New Agers who believe in the so-called "Urantia Book."

The "revelations" contained in this 2097-page book come from alleged extraterrestrial spirit beings such as Melchizedek of Nebadon, Bagriel of Salvington, and the Chief of the Seraphim. The book sets out to offer to those who live on Earth ("Urantia," as it is known to these extraterrestrials) "the finest world view of religion available to contemporary man."[16]

The Urantia Book claims that humankind's deepest need is not atonement for sin, but rather a consciousness expanded to realize the fatherhood of God and the brotherhood of man. The book teaches that Jesus is not uniquely the Son of God, for there are allegedly some 700,000 Creator-Sons in the universe (Jesus was number 611,121). Jesus differs from us not in kind, but in degree. Christ was divine as we all are. He was able to perfect His divinity by His seventh incarnation.

The book also denies Christ's blood atonement and His bodily resurrection from the dead. It blatantly sets forth what Scripture calls "another Jesus" (2 Corinthians 11:4) and "a gospel other than the one we preached" (Galatians 1:8). Just about every cardinal tenet of the Christian religion has been dismissed by the "space brothers" who wrote the Urantia Book. Does this appear to be a demonic agenda to you, as it does to me?

The Easternizing of Western Religion

Another way we can illustrate this demonic agenda is to point to the current Easternizing of Western religion. Did you know that according to New Agers, the space brothers aboard UFOs are busy working on the religious scene, and they are credited for the growth of the Eastern religions on American soil since the 1960s?

A New Age seeress, Kathleen Karter, was interviewed on this issue, and her comments on how the "space brothers" are influencing the religious scene are highly revealing:

> *Question:* What do you think their [the UFOs'] influence is?
>
> *Ms. Karter:* It's a spiritual one, primarily. Right now I feel the spiritual influences are playing upon the Earth very forcefully. I think that, as we enter the Aquarian Age, man will undergo more experiences with UFOs.
>
> *Question:* Are the UFOs teaching us, helping us, in our spiritual evolution?
>
> *Ms. Karter:* Yes, especially here in the West. I feel the West is becoming the East, and the East is becoming the West. I feel that the East has already gone through a period of heavy interaction with UFOs. They might not have appeared to them as UFOs, they may have manifested as divine beings.

But now it is the West's turn to undergo a strong period of interaction with UFO intelligence.[17]

In other words, it is now time for people in the West (in the United States) to become enlightened, as those in the East (the Hindus) already have. This fits right in with the rest of the New Age movement, with its heavy emphasis on Eastern religious elements—including the teachings that all is God, all is one, death is not the end, and reincarnation is real. As one New Ager put it, we are presently headed toward "an impending New Age wherein mankind will attain a new consciousness, a new awareness, and a higher state."[18]

New Age Reinterpretations of the End Times

Have you ever wondered how the biblical rapture and tribulation period are going to be explained by those left behind and still living on Earth in the end times? (The "rapture" is that event in which Christ will snatch Christians off the Earth prior to the beginning of the "tribulation period." The "tribulation" is a seven-year period in the end times during which God's judgments will be poured out on the Earth.) Current New Age literature indicates that at least one of the strategies the powers of darkness have concocted to explain away these end-time events relates to UFOs.

In a capsule, New Age UFO enthusiasts tell us that according to the space brothers aboard UFOs, a great time of cleansing is coming upon the earth. It will be a very difficult time for humankind to endure. It will be a time of tribulation. Following this time of cleansing will come a glorious planet-wide Utopia.

New Ager David Icke believes that extraterrestrials are arriving on Earth in large numbers to help us "make the giant leap in evolution into the Aquarian Age, when humankind, or those who are evolved enough to meet the challenge, will rise out of the abyss at last." Indeed, Icke says, "they are here to guide us through tremendously difficult times with love, wisdom, and understanding, and we ignore them and reject what they say to our cost."[19] An examination of UFO literature indicates that Icke's view is not unique.

Brad Steiger, another New Ager, comments:

> In the last 30 years the extraterrestrials have been accelerating their interaction with us in preparation for a fast-approaching time of transition and transformation. This period, we have been told, will be a difficult one; and for generations our prophets and revelators have been referring to it as The Great Cleansing, Judgment Day, Armageddon. But we have been promised that, after a season of cataclysmic changes on the Earth plane, a New Age consciousness will suffuse the planet.[20]

Steiger goes on to say:

> Contactees have been told that the Space Beings hope to guide Earth to a period of great unification, when all races will shun discriminatory separations and all of mankind will recognize its responsibility to every other life form existing on the planet. The Space Beings also seek to bring about a single, unified government, which will conduct itself on spiritual principles and permit all of its citizens to grow constructively in "love."[21]

The New Age Exodus

Before the time of cleansing comes upon the earth, we are told that many of the enlightened people of the earth will be evacuated by UFOs and saved from the troubles to come. The term "rapture" is used by New Age UFOlogists to describe this event. The "raptured" people will allegedly live on another planet as the time of cleansing unfolds on Earth. Gabriel Green, founder of one of the largest UFO groups in America (the Amalgamated Flying Saucer Club), tells us:

> If Armageddon comes, so will the aliens, swooping down in spaceships to evacuate one-tenth of the population in what Christians call "the rapture." . . . Only one-tenth of the population will be spiritually qualified to live in an environment of harmony, and there are some limitations on their [the extraterrestrials'] ability to provide for us, to house us and so forth.[22]

Another New Ager who claims to have received psychic revelations said he was told that—

> a period of cleansing was necessary before Earth could pass into the Aquarian Age. A series of cataclysms would precede the planet's tilting on its axis. Such an adjustment of the axis would destroy the Earth in its physical sense, but the Space Brothers would remove the Chosen and return them to Earth after the planet had once again "crystallized" and been spiritually, as well as materially, restructured.[23]

Timothy Green Beckley, author of *Psychic and UFO Revelations in the Last Days*, researched this issue and consulted many New Age psychics. He tells us:

> It became quite clear that there is an understanding among many mystics and sensitives that massive

UFO landings will take place and will take up a select few just in the nick of time. This same belief is worldwide and comes from many groups and individuals who claim they are receiving regular messages from highly evolved beings who reside elsewhere than our planet.[24]

Beckley interviewed one New Age psychic named Jane who I found particularly interesting:

"I have been a practicing psychic for several years, but have only recently gotten into space channeling," she explains. Jane had a very moving UFO experience in lower Manhattan and shortly thereafter she started to receive some rather remarkable communications which include end-time prophecies.

"I've been told that there will be a landing in a large flat area of either Arizona or New Mexico," Jane says. "I have no idea of the actual number of craft that will land, but those that do touch down will be used to evacuate people into space when the earthquakes and other natural disturbances become too much to handle."

In October, 1978 Jane received through automatic writing that a communications network is now being set up to assist in an evacuation. "I've also experienced a series of dreams in which I was told that at one point our sky is going to be filled up with spaceships. I was further shown that there will be much turmoil and confusion and there will be buildings collapsing. A psychic saw me climbing into a spaceship that will hold up to 300 people, and I have felt that when there is an evacuation, I will be among those to be taken off this planet."[25]

How many New Age "faithful" will be evacuated in this "rapture"? As noted earlier, one New Age leader estimates that 10 percent of the population will be taken up. Other New Agers suggest a much smaller estimate. One representative New Age psychic says, "We would estimate that altogether perhaps 140,000 to 170,000 people will be lifted up and taken off the planet."[26]

Now keep in mind that this is a basic New Age scenario of the end times; there are many variations and differences in detail among different New Age groups. But what I have presented is a basic skeleton view that individual New Age groups put their own "flesh" on—that is, they all add their own unique twists to how all this unfolds in the end times.

For example, following the time of cleansing, many New Agers believe that those who were raptured will be brought back to Earth by UFOs. Some New Agers believe that for those who are left to stay on Earth for the entire duration of the time of cleansing, the UFOs will render assistance in every way they can, so that they will survive. Others believe that the time of cleansing will in fact *destroy* the rest of humanity. In this variation, the planet itself will become healed following the time of cleansing. Sometime later the human beings who had been raptured will be brought back to Earth by UFOs in order to re-populate the Earth (kind of like Noah and his family following the flood).

One New Ager's Story

Perhaps the New Age embrace of UFOs can best be illustrated in the life of a former New Ager—Randall Baer. After Baer became a Christian, he wrote a book entitled *Inside the New Age Nightmare*. In this book, Baer said that over 75 percent of all New Agers hold to an absolutely unshakable belief in the reality of UFOs.[27] Baer discerningly noted that "the strong upsurge in this trend [of belief in UFOs] also parallels the crystal

97

craze and the huge increases in channeling activities in the mid-to-late 80s."[28]

Baer claims that among New Agers the question of whether UFOs are real is rarely contested or questioned. "This belief is part and parcel of much, though not all, of the New Age mentality. UFOs are involved quite heavily in their concepts of the world's deliverance from a time of suffering and tribulation into an enlightened 'One World United Government' (that is, the New Age)."[29]

What is the purpose of the UFO visitations? Baer says that when he was a New Ager he believed (along with other New Agers) that these space brothers had come from a variety of galaxies, and that they were part of a collective "Intergalactic Space Federation." They were believed to be working together to assist planets like Earth to go through a "purification process" preceding a quantum leap into a new evolutionary stage of human development—a New Age of "Heaven-on-earth."[30] Often the message brought by the alien visitors involved several key factors:

- Man is not alone in the solar system. He has space brothers, and they have come to Earth to reach him and to teach him.
- The space brothers have advanced information that they wish to impart to their weaker brethren.
- The space brothers want man to join an intergalactic spiritual federation.
- The space brothers are here to teach, to help awaken man's spirit, to help man rise to higher levels of vibration, so that he may be ready to enter new dimensions.
- Man stands now in the transitional period before the dawn of a New Age.[31]

New Agers believe that extraterrestrials are *already* heavily involved in helping humanity. As Baer puts it:

> Most New Agers hold firmly to the view that hundreds, if not thousands, of UFOs already are deeply involved in rendering aid to planet Earth in subtle but highly significant ways. But, because of a kind of "prime non-interference directive" (like on *Star Trek*), the extraterrestrials cannot intervene directly or render explicit assistance until humanity is ready for their help. These extraterrestrials are believed to have a highly evolved spiritual philosophy (akin to New Age philosophy) and extremely advanced technologies, both of which form the foundation for the New Age One World Order.[32]

Baer's comments on the "prime non-interference directive" is quite common in New Age circles. For example, Timothy Green Beckley, in his book *Psychic and UFO Revelations in the Last Days,* writes:

> There is a cosmic law against interfering in the affairs of others, so they are not allowed to help us directly even though they could easily do so. We must make our own choice of our own free will. Present trends indicate a series of events which may require the help of these people and they stand by ready and willing to render that help. In fact, they have already helped us a great deal, along lines which do not interfere with our freedom of choice. In time, when certain events have transpired, and we are so oriented that we can accept these people from elsewhere, they will meet

us freely on the common ground of mutual understanding and trust, and we will be able to learn
from them and bring about the Golden Age all
men everywhere desire deep within their hearts.[33]

Randall Baer recalls how his mentors told him and his
New Age associates to start calling out in their meditations to
the space brothers, who allegedly were highly advanced extraterrestrial intelligences stationed in this solar system. These
space brothers had come from a variety of galaxies and were
here to bring enlightenment.[34]

Baer concedes that all this may sound a bit "wacky" to a
normal person. However, he says millions of New Agers are
absolutely convinced that these things are true. "In fact, in
most New Age circles, a person is considered a bit weird or
'out of it' if he doesn't believe in all this."[35]

Satan the Great Counterfeiter

It is fascinating to read what all these New Agers are saying
about the coming "evacuation" of Earth. This is very clearly a
counterfeit doctrine that mimics the orthodox Christian doctrine of the rapture.

It was Augustine who called the devil *Simius Dei*—"the
ape of God." Satan is the great counterfeiter; he mimics God in
many ways. In fact, it would seem that the principal tactic Satan
uses to attack God and His program in general is to offer a counterfeit kingdom and program. This is hinted at in 2 Corinthians
11:14, which makes reference to Satan masquerading as an
"angel of light."

In what ways does Satan act as "the ape of God"? Consider the following:

• Satan has his own *church*—the "synagogue of
Satan" (Revelation 2:9).

- Satan has his own *ministers*—ministers of darkness who bring false sermons (2 Corinthians 11:4,5).

- Satan has formulated his own *system of theology*—called "things taught by demons" (1 Timothy 4:1; see also Revelation 2:24).

- Satan's ministers proclaim his *gospel*—"a gospel other than the one we preached to you" (Galatians 1:7,8).

- Satan has his own *throne* (Revelation 13:2) and his own worshipers (13:4).

- Satan inspires *false Christs* and self-constituted *messiahs* (Matthew 24:4,5).

- Satan employs *false teachers* who bring in "destructive heresies" (2 Peter 2:1).

- Satan sends out *false prophets* (Matthew 24:11).

- Satan sponsors *false apostles* who imitate the true apostles (2 Corinthians 11:13).

In view of such mimicking, we must conclude that Satan's plan and purposes have been, are now, and always will be to seek to establish a rival rule to God's kingdom. He is promoting a system of which he is the head and which stands in opposition to God and His rule in the universe.

The things I have documented in this chapter have caused my friend (and Christian UFO researcher) William Alnor to legitimately ask:

> Could it be that the similar end-times scenarios being spewed in the form of messages from the space brothers are deliberate attempts to fool humankind

about Bible prophecy in the very era of Christ's return? Could the benevolent space brothers that the New Agers talk about actually be some of the "angels of light" deliberately sent by Satan to deceive mankind whom the apostle Paul warned the early Christian church about (2 Corinthians 11:14)?[36]

The discerning Christian must wonder the same.

Alnor's conclusion is chilling: "I have concluded that the emerging religion of the UFOnauts is part of a diabolical program of disinformation—perhaps the greatest in history." Indeed, "it involves a clever counterfeit of the Christian message and a retranslation of future events as seen by most in the church today."[37]

UFO Cults in the New Age

The ships are expected to land first in the Bermuda Triangle. One of their first benevolent acts will be to recover the libraries of Atlantis and Lemuria.

> —Researcher Diana Tumminia and
> R. George Kirkpatrick[1]

No book on UFOs would be complete without a chapter on the most popular of the UFO cults of our day. In what follows, I will briefly illustrate how four specific New Age groups—the Unarius Academy of Science, the Raelian Movement, the Aetherius Society, and the Heaven's Gate cult—have made the UFO phenomenon a big part of their belief systems. You will notice both similarities and differences among them. You will also notice that each offers a satanic counterfeit explanation for the end times.

The Unarius Academy of Science

Unarius stands for UNiversal ARticulate Interdimensional Understanding of Science, and was founded in 1954 by the late Ernest and Ruth Norman.[2] According to members of the Unarius Academy of Science, UFO starships are going to touch down on planet Earth in the year 2001. Some 67 acres of land have been purchased in the mountains of San Diego, California, to accommodate the landings. Understandably, Unarius has been the subject of numerous news reports in both the print and broadcast media.

The starting point for any discussion of Unarius is the fact that its founders, Ernest and Ruth Norman, had a history of occultic involvement. In fact, Ruth met Ernest at a psychic convention in 1954. Prior to this time, Ernest had worked in spiritualist churches (churches that engage in *spiritism*—communicating with the dead). Ernest engaged in a psychic reading the first time he met Ruth, and "discovered" that in a previous incarnation she had been the pharaoh's daughter that rescued Moses in the bulrushes. Ernest later psychically "discovered" that they were also Jesus and Mary Magdalene in a previous incarnation.[3]

Using clairvoyance, Ernest claimed to receive psychic "transmissions" from Mars and Venus. Subsequent channelings revealed to him that there were "spiritual planets"—involving not just Mars and Venus but also Eros, Orion, Muse, Elysium, and Hermes. Transmissions indicated that there were advanced learning centers on these spiritual planets, and that Ascended Masters living at such centers would "transmit" knowledge to adepts like Ernest. One unique teaching of Unarius is that students who are asleep may actually have out-of-body experiences and "astral travel" to these centers where the great masters teach.[4]

Based on the transmissions received by Ernest, Unarius members believe that this 2001 alien landing will usher in a Utopia—a golden age of "logic and reason." The space brothers aboard the UFOs will bring with them higher knowledge and various gifts of technology. Unique to Unarius is the suggestion that these UFO starships will land *on top of each other*, forming a saucer tower of sorts. These saucers, each from one of 33 other worlds, will invite earthlings to join their Interplanetary Confederation.

When I saw the film *Independence Day*, I thought *those* flying saucers were big (about a mile in diameter). But the flying saucers described by the Unarius Academy of Science are even bigger—as much as five miles in diameter. According to Unarius literature, each of these ships will bring 1000 scientists to the Earth, with a total of 33,000 interplanetary scientists. These scientists will all work for the betterment of humankind.

Each level of the multilevel saucer tower will be devoted to a different field of science, we are told. The incredible technology brought by these scientists will serve to solve all of humankind's economic and social problems. This means that earthlings will no longer have to spend their time earning a living. Now they can devote themselves to education and serving man. There will even be new forms of learning involving special techno-caps that can be put on one's head in order to read "a book a night."[5]

It is interesting to note that such mysterious topics as the Bermuda Triangle and Atlantis are a part of the Unarius scenario. Prior to landing in San Diego, the UFO ships will allegedly land in the Bermuda Triangle on a submerged but soon-to-rise land mass that once was home to Atlantis. We are told:

> The ships are expected to land first in the Bermuda Triangle. One of their first benevolent acts will be to recover the libraries of Atlantis and Lemuria. The contents of these libraries, said to be on thin metal plates somewhere in the debris of the sunken continents, will be given back to the Earth people. The Space Brothers have plans to train technicians with this knowledge in order to build

crystal and gold computers and other wondrous technology.[6]

Atlantis, of course, is the legendary lost continent that is believed by many to have sunk as a result of a natural disaster.[7] Occultic literature is brimming with references to Atlantis, with constant mention of the extremely advanced and enlightened society that once lived there. Some occultists, particularly those in the New Age movement, have speculated that this "lost culture" was actually a group of alien beings from outer space.[8]

William Proctor, a Unarius teacher, tells us that the space brothers will teach human beings the way to peace and harmony. "They will speak from their experiences to end hatred and disease."[9] When the aliens arrive, there will be no more wars and no more suffering, Proctor says. "It will be proof for the skeptics. It will be rapturous, and it will be heavenly."[10]

According to Unarius literature, these alien scientists will also allegedly build a magnificent university and medical center that will be open to all people of the Earth without charge. The space brothers will provide advanced healing machines to earthlings. We are told that these machines will have the capability of examining the past lives of people in order to bring healing in the present:

> The hospital will be able to heal mental as well as physical diseases with the help of the "psychic anatomy viewer." According to Unarian science, information about past lives leads to healing. As such, the "psychic anatomy viewer" will X-ray the "electronic body," a term used to describe the past-life karma as it is held in the electromagnetic memory of the body. This machine will reveal any "malformations" and the exact time they occurred

in a past life. With this information, a person is then thought to be able to release his or her problem.

For example, if a person injured another during battle in a past life on Atlantis, the guilt would still be found in the "electronic body." According to Unarius, this might cause any number of illnesses which would heal upon receipt of this datum. This "psychic anatomy viewer" is expected to empty all hospitals, prisons, and asylums. Drug abuse and alcoholism will be unheard of in the age the new science will create.[11]

Presently there are 90,000 people on a mailing list for Unarius books, literature, and pins.[12] The center's video programs have aired since 1978 on 25 cable stations throughout the United States. It is claimed that about 500,000 people worldwide have gotten the Unarius message.[13] It is sad to realize that so many people are open to such teaching.

The Raelian Movement

The Raelian movement was founded in 1973 by a French race-car driver and journalist known as "Rael" (his birth name was Claude Vorilhon, but he was named "Rael" by aliens). Rael founded the movement following an alleged encounter he had with some space aliens while walking through a volcanic mountain range in France.[14]

The backdrop to this encounter, however, goes back much further. According to Raelian literature, Rael (Vorilhon) was born as a hybrid being, having a human for a mother but an alien for a father:

Just after the first atomic bomb explosion of Hiroshima in 1945, the Elohim [aliens] selected

Marie Colette Vorilhon to be his mother. She was born in Ambert on the 22nd of October 1922. On the 25th of December 1945 they took her inside a UFO and inseminated her. They then erased it from her memory so as not to psychologically unbalance her, and on the 30th of September 1946 Rael was born from this union.[15]

It was after Vorilhon grew up that he had his first alien encounter. He describes the aliens as being about four feet in height, with long dark hair, almond-shaped eyes, and olive skin.[16] These beings, according to Rael's story, entrusted him with a message: Out of all the human beings on earth, Rael was the one chosen to spread "the greatest message ever revealed to humanity," and he was to be an apostle of a New World Order.[17] The message entrusted to him is said to answer the existential questions that have plagued human beings since the beginning of man's existence: *Who am I? Where did I come from? Why am I here?*

These aliens allegedly told Rael that humans were "implanted" on the Earth by advanced extraterrestrial scientists known as the "Elohim." (Rael wrongly claims that *Elohim* literally means "those who came from the sky.") The Elohim allegedly created humanity from DNA in their laboratories. In fact, we are told, this is what the book of Genesis was really talking about in its early chapters:

> In the book of Genesis of the original Bible, it does not say "God," in fact it uses the word "Elohim," which in ancient Hebrew is a plural and means "those who come from the sky." Thus Genesis is a written account of how people from another planet created all life on earth. The messages dictated to Rael explain how the Elohim used their

mastery of genetics to scientifically create life from inert chemicals using DNA.[18]

The alien that appeared to Rael told him that "we were the ones who made all life on earth; you mistook us for Gods, we were at the origin of your main religions. Now that you are mature enough to understand this, we would like to enter official contact through an embassy."[19]

Rael says he is the last of "40 prophets," each of whom was crossbred between the Elohim and mortal women. As a prophet, Rael's task is allegedly to warn humankind that since the explosion of the first atomic bomb in the year 1945, humanity has been in the "Age of Apocalypse." We now have a huge collective choice to make. We can either destroy ourselves with nuclear bombs, or we can make a leap into planetary consciousness that will then qualify us to receive the scientific knowledge of our space forefathers.

The Raelians are "millenarian" in the sense that they are presently preparing for the descent of UFOs around the turn of the millennium. These UFOs will be carrying the Elohim as well as the other 39 immortal prophets (including the likes of Jesus, Buddha, Mohammed, and the Mormon prophet Joseph Smith). Rael has been assigned to build an embassy in Jerusalem by the year 2025 where the creators (the Elohim) can live and hand down to us their scientific heritage as well as the secret of eternal life: *cloning*.[20] "Cloning is the secret of eternal life. Cloning will make the life of people better by curing genetic diseases."[21]

This hope of "eternal life" even involves rituals. Researcher Susan Jean Palmer explains it this way:

> Denying the existence of God or the soul, Rael presents as the only hope of immortality a regeneration through science, and to this end members

participate in four annual festivals so that the Elo-him can fly overhead and register the Raelians' DNA codes on their machines. This initiation ritual, called "the transmission of the cellular plan," promises a kind of immortality through cloning. New initiates sign a contract which permits a mortician to cut out a piece of bone in their forehead (the "third eye") which is stored in ice awaiting the descent of the Elohim.[22]

Why is an embassy necessary for the alien visitors? Raelian literature tells us that "without the neutrality of an embassy, free air space and an official welcome, an unannounced and undesired landing would have enormous political, economic and social repercussions with disastrous consequences worldwide."[23] Moreover, the alien visitors do not wish "to sanction any government, religion or ideology other than that of the Raelian Movement, by contacting another building first. Thus they will only come when we build their embassy, such is their love and respect for us."[24]

Rael's book, *The Message Given to Me by Extraterrestrials,* is claimed to be a world bestseller, translated into 22 languages. The Raelians boast 35,000 members in 84 countries.[25] The movement has more than a dozen offices throughout the world—including ones in Japan, Africa, Switzerland, Mexico, Canada, and three in the United States: Los Angeles, Las Vegas, and Miami.[26]

The Aetherius Society

The Aetherius Society is "a worldwide Spiritual Brotherhood dedicated to the salvation and enlightenment of mankind."[27] The worldview of the society includes such things as a belief in clairvoyant powers, reincarnation, karma, the Ascended Masters (perfect beings including Jesus, St. Germain, Kuthumi, and

El Morya), the Great White Brotherhood, mantras, and the "occult secrets of Jesus."[28] This group is unquestionably one of the more popular of the New Age UFO groups.

The Aetherius Society was founded in 1954 by George King, a student of Yoga. While living in London, King was informed by a "cosmic brotherhood" that he should prepare himself, for he was to become the voice of the "Interplanetary Parliament." Indeed, he was to be the "Primary Terrestrial Mental Channel."[29] King had previously been "taught by an advanced Master from the East how to obtain telepathic rapport with the Cosmic Masters."[30]

A little over a week after this initial prophetic message, King claims he was visited by a "space master" who entered his apartment even while the door was locked. The "master" gave King instructions in advanced Yoga. From this initial meeting, King developed a rapport with Master Aetherius, who resided on the planet Venus (a spiritual planet).[31]

King says that in 1958 he came into contact with the Master Jesus, who also lived on the planet Venus. (We are told that "after his resurrection and ascension, Jesus went to live on Venus, where, in the company of other religious founders such as Buddha and Ramakrishna, he continues his concern for the enlightenment of earthlings. Jesus is one of the Great Masters and not the sole son of God."[32]) According to King's story, the Master Jesus gave King the first chapter of his *Aquarian Age Bible.* King also continued to receive "transmissions" from Master Aetherius, which were then published in a magazine entitled *Aetherius Speaks.*[33]

The Cosmic Masters, we are told, sincerely desire to help humanity. "The Cosmic Masters have been given permission to increase their help to mankind at this pivotal time to help our world choose the right road. To help mankind help himself and to guide us towards the New Age."[34] The Masters seek to give us "cosmic knowledge" and increase our "spiritual energy."[35]

Presently the Aetherius Society expends great efforts to study UFO visitations to planet Earth. Aetherius members say that the UFO spacecraft, normally functioning at a high vibratory rate, occasionally *lower* their vibratory rate so that humans on earth can see them.[36] Like many others within the UFO movement, members of the Aetherius Society believe that the governments of the world have conspired to cover up reports of actual contacts with beings from outer space.[37]

The Society teaches that the entire universe is a battleground between the opposing forces of good and evil. The battles between these forces are allegedly fought on both the astral and physical planes. (The "astral plane" is allegedly a kind of etheric spirit-plane of existence.) These forces are said to advance from planet to planet by spaceships.

> Because Terra [Earth] is so underdeveloped spiritually, it could become easy prey and fall to an all-out assault by the forces of evil, led by a group with the ominous sounding name of the Black Magicians. What saves planet earth from destruction is the constant and repeated intervention on her behalf by the space masters.[38]

Travel between planets is made possible by very fast spacecraft that use a special kind of energy. "Physical flights between planets very distant from each other is done using a special energy, which makes it able to fly with the speed of light. People on higher developed planets are able to do this by the help of thought-power."[39] Indeed, "cosmic energy is collected in special generators, which is then controlled by very strong thought-power."[40]

Aetherius Society members believe in the existence of an "Interplanetary Federation." This federation seeks to help Earth, but the inhabitants of Earth must "raise their consciousness" in order for this to happen. The Aetherius Society Web Page on the Internet contains the following message received by a society member from an entity "residing in the spiritual dimensions":

> The Interplanetary Federation is a union of about 7 million planets. This large number will ensure you that the help needed is available. But I will repeat: the condition for receiving this help is a leap in the consciousness of the inhabitants of your planet, as a whole. We cannot help in a rate faster than the progress of this collective consciousness of yours. Therefore my very first advice to you is to raise your level of consciousness and help others to do the same; to work with your attitudes . . . in relation to the cosmic view and the conception of the Earth as a living organism.[41]

Beings from this federation are also in contact with the animal world on planet Earth. Indeed, "dolphins and whales with their highly developed sensory and sonar system are the perfect receivers of signals from other planets, their inhabitants, and their spaceships, as well as they also can use these senses to receive impulses from the spiritual world."[42] We must keep in mind that "no other creatures on Earth have so strong telepathic abilities as especially certain groups of dolphins."[43]

According to Aetherius literature, King's mother, Mary, met with Jesus aboard a spacecraft in 1959. Jesus allegedly acknowledged that her son George had been chosen as a leader among human beings in this New Age.[44]

Some members of the Aetherius Society believe that Mary King was actually the biblical Mary in a previous life. In a way, then, this means that George King is a form of Christ at His second coming.[45]

King and the Aetherius Society are presently "calling humanity to make a decision on behalf of a new and imminent age of utopia."[46]

Heaven's Gate

By now it is well-known that the 39 devotees of the UFO cult Heaven's Gate killed themselves during Easter week in Rancho Santa Fe, California. Cult members were thoroughly convinced that following their deaths they would rendezvous with an alien spaceship that was believed to be riding piggyback on the wake of Comet Hale-Bopp. There were no signs of violence when their bodies were discovered dressed in black and shrouded with diamond-shaped purple cloths. They all died willingly, fully convinced of the truth of their beliefs.[47]

As one examines the theology behind the actions of this cult, one is confronted with the truly bizarre. According to Heaven's Gate literature, some 2000 years ago the "Kingdom Level Above Human" appointed a representative to preach the "Kingdom of God" to earthlings. This being allegedly inhabited a "container" called Jesus. Jesus came to enlighten us as to how we too could evolve to the Kingdom Level Above Human. Jesus was subsequently killed by people who eventually turned His teachings into a "watered-down Country Club religion" (Christianity).

Two beings by the name of "Ti" and "Do," however, were then appointed as the Kingdom Level's successor-representatives to Jesus. They are said to be the "two witnesses" prophesied in the book of Revelation.

As a backdrop, Heaven's Gate was founded by a man and a woman—Marshall Applewhite, who said his spiritual name was "Do," and Bonnie Nettles, who used the spiritual name "Ti." (Ti died of cancer in 1985.)[48] The two had met in a hospital. Bonnie was a nurse, while Marshall was a mental patient. They soon came to believe that their bodies were inhabited by extraterrestrials from the kingdom of heaven. They were convinced they were the two witnesses of Revelation (Revelation 11:3ff.), and eventually came to be called "the two" among their followers.[49]

Ti and Do traveled around the country and left calling cards at churches. They eventually accumulated some students. Soon they realized that they were in some ways like Bo and Peep, looking for their lost sheep. This is why they called themselves Bo and Peep for a time.[50]

They taught their students that the only way to enter into the kingdom of heaven (which involved leaving Earth on a UFO spacecraft and going to a higher plane of existence) was to renounce all human possessions—including one's sex, drugs, alcohol, birth names, family, fortune, and material assets. By renouncing these things, they were told, they could ascend to space, shedding their "containers" (bodies) and enter into "God's kingdom."

In Heaven's Gate theology, the *soul* is a "deposit" or "seed" that is placed in "vehicles" (mammalian bodies, sometimes called "plants") that serve as "containers" that make possible the evolution of that soul into the Level Beyond Human. After the souls are evolved, the containers can be shed and the soul can move on to a higher level of existence—in this case, with the assistance of a UFO. "We fully desire, expect, and look forward to boarding a spacecraft from the Next Level very soon . . . . There is no doubt in our mind that our being 'picked up' is inevitable in the very near future."[51]

Heaven's Gate is properly categorized as a "millenarian cult." This group attracted followers by promising escape from expected cataclysmic events that supposedly will signal the end of this millennium. They ultimately "escaped" these cataclysmic events by committing suicide. *Time* magazine reported that "students of the millennium and historians of the bizarre have long been predicting such a catastrophic event in the twilight years of the 20th century, duly noting the rise in the number of obscure cults and the increasingly fevered pitch of their rantings."[52]

It is important to note that members of Heaven's Gate do not necessarily consider suicide a bad thing. In their theology, the final act of "metamorphosis" (separation from the human kingdom) is the so-called "disconnect" (separation) from the "human container" (body) in order to be released from the human environment for a higher level of existence. In their belief, they thought they would all rendezvous in the "clouds" (in a giant UFO mothership) for the journey to the "Kingdom of God."[53]

The Heaven's Gate teaching that the body is a mere "container" for one's spirit strongly resembles the teachings of the Gnostics in the second and third centuries A.D. Christian apologist Douglas Groothuis comments:

> The Gnostics, like Heaven's Gate, believed that they were among a small group of enlightened beings who were too good for this poor world. They possessed a divine spark within a prison of corrupted flesh, while all orthodox Christians were just wallowing in ignorance. Only the Gnostics (taken from the Greek word *gnosis* for knowledge) were in-the-know.[54]

Some newspaper reports tried to tie Heaven's Gate to Christianity. But such an understanding displays the greatest level of ignorance. Like many cults, Heaven's Gate members employed some Christian terminology, but they poured their own cultic meanings into those words. They believed in a counterfeit Jesus who preached a counterfeit gospel which, sadly, yielded a counterfeit salvation (a UFO salvation). What a tragedy that 39 people followed one man to the point of death, believing that they would rendezvous aboard a UFO!

Here we have a combination of doctrinal lies and subsequent death. I can think of a verse in Scripture where these two elements are combined. Jesus, speaking to some Jews who were seeking to kill Him, said: "You belong to your father, the devil, and you want to carry out your father's desire. He was a *murderer* from the beginning, *not holding to the truth,* for there is *no truth* in him. When he *lies,* he speaks his native language, for he is a *liar* and the *father of lies*" (John 8:44, emphasis added). Can there be any doubt that the theology of Heaven's Gate is rooted in the work of Satan?

— 8 —

The Occult Connection

*In recent years . . . the report of paranormal events in
connection with close encounters with UFOs seems to
have become the rule rather than the exception.*
       —Jacques Vallee[1]

Most UFO sightings, as I noted in an earlier chapter,
can be easily dismissed as mistakenly identified
planets, rocket launchings, weather balloons, and
various atmospheric phenomena. Sometimes, however, sightings cannot be so easily explained. Indeed, the Air Force's
Project Blue Book was not able to provide a rationale for 700
out of 12,600 cases of sightings between 1947 and 1969, when
the project was abandoned.[2] Somewhere between 5 and 10
percent of all UFO sightings remain truly *unidentified*.[3]

We will examine in detail the occultic connection to *abduction* experiences in the next chapter. The present chapter is
introductory in nature, and its sole goal is to point to the connection between occultism and UFO phenomena in general.
This connection has been recognized by numerous authorities
in the field. Brooks Alexander of the Spiritual Counterfeits
Project, for example, notes that many of the reported cases of

UFO contact "show some kind of occult involvement prior to initial UFO contact."[4] Christian researcher John Weldon likewise notes that "UFO contactees often have a history of psychic abilities or an interest in the occult."[5]

Standard Tools of the Occult

In seeking to unravel who these "aliens" are, it is highly revealing that while UFOs typically do not respond to aerial pursuit or standard approaches (such as radio contact), the standard tools of the occult have been claimed to establish contact in innumerable cases.[6] Those who successfully make "contact" are those typically involved in one or more of the following: trance states, seances, clairvoyance, spiritism, automatic handwriting, peering into crystals, levitation, out-of-body experiences, and the like.[7]

The above terms may be new to you, so allow me to explain.

• *Automatic handwriting* is "the phenomenon in spiritualism whereby a medium begins to write without apparent awareness."[11] The source of such writing is believed to be from a dead person's spirit or a paranormal entity (such as an "alien").

• *Clairvoyance* involves the mental "seeing" of physical objects or events at a distance by psychic means. It involves the ability to perceive things beyond physical reality. Sometimes the term is used to refer to the psychic ability to "see" and describe future events.[9]

• *Levitation* refers to the phenomenon of "free floating," in which an animate or inanimate object is suspended in the air with no apparent means of support.[13] An example of this phenomenon involves seances in which the spiritualist's table lifts off the ground, indicating the presence of spirit beings or paranormal entities.

• *Out-of-body experiences,* also called *astral projection,* involves the body remaining stationary while one's soul or spirit allegedly leaves the body and travels around to different locations—even (so occultists claim) into outer space. Occultists often speak of a thin gray cord that remains connected between one's soul and the body.

• *Peering into crystals* (or a crystal ball) is a form of divination or fortune-telling that involves seeking paranormal information or knowledge of the future by means of a crystal. "Gazing into the glass, the clairvoyant enters into a trance-like state and is able to view future events."[12]

• A *seance* is a meeting of a group of people who attempt to communicate with the spirit world or with souls of departed people through a medium. Mediums often use the assistance of a "guide," a Ouija board, and automatic handwriting. A *guide* is a spirit present during a seance that offers advice and guidance—often considered to be a guru or priest from centuries past. A *Ouija board* is a game-board containing numbers and letters with a pointer that a "visiting spirit" can use to communicate a message from the spirit world by guiding the hand of the medium. (*Automatic handwriting* is defined above.)[8]

• *Spiritism,* also called *channeling,* may be defined as "the practice of attempting communication with departed human or extrahuman intelligences (usually nonphysical) through the agency of a human medium, with the intent of receiving paranormal information and/or having direct experience of metaphysical realities."[10]

• A *trance state* involves an altered state of consciousness, a sleeplike condition that enables the subject's body to be used by a discarnate spirit or paranormal entity (such as an "alien"). In such states telepathic communication is often said to take place.

I want to emphasize that *all* of these occultic practices are condemned by God (see Deuteronomy 18:10-12). And *all* of these—either in isolation or taken together—can lead a person into an encounter of some kind with a "UFO," possibly even an "abduction" (more on this in the next chapter). *This is extremely dangerous activity and is strictly off-limits for the Christian.*

Christian UFO investigator David Wimbish, who has engaged in significant research into the UFO phenomenon, has suggested that not only can the occult lead one to have a "UFO" encounter, but interest in UFOs can actually draw one *into* the occult: "Many UFO investigators have followed a path that has taken them directly into the world of the occult. They believe they are rediscovering ancient spiritual truths and uncovering new realities about the universe. It's more likely that they are getting involved with some ancient deceptions."[14] Indeed, the UFO phenomenon "has led many to experiment with astral projection, to believe in reincarnation, and to get involved in other practices that directly oppose the historic teachings of the Christian church."[15]

Jacques Vallee, well-known French UFO investigator, made the following comments regarding the occult connection to UFO phenomena:

> A few investigators . . . have suggested both in public statements and in private conversations with me that there may be a link between UFO events and "occult" phenomena.
>
> At first view, the very suggestion of such a link is disturbing to a scientist. However . . . the phenomena reported by [UFO] witnesses involve poltergeist effects, levitation, psychic control, healing, and out-of-body experiences . . . familiar [themes] . . . [of] occult literature . . . found in the teachings of the Rosicrucian Order . . . which have inspired not only the witchcraft revival, but also

... "psychic" writers and ... "scientific parapsychologists."[16]

For a non-Christian, secular scientist such as Jacques Vallee to make such a statement is significant. Vallee has personally investigated countless UFO sightings, and his comments are based on years of firsthand observation. Vallee concludes that "in recent years ... the report of paranormal events in connection with close encounters with UFOs seems to have become the rule rather than the exception."[17]

The occult connection to UFO phenomena is certainly verified by the UFO reports that have come out of the former Soviet Union. In fact, because of all the UFO stories coming from that part of the world, Vallee decided to pay a visit there and ended up writing a book entitled *UFO Chronicles of the Soviet Union.*

Vallee discovered that cosmonauts, some of whom had reported UFO phenomena, are typically trained by parapsychologists and are also trained in Eastern meditation.[18] For those of you not familiar with the term, a parapsychologist is a person concerned with the investigation of evidence for paranormal psychological phenomena such as telepathy, clairvoyance, and psychokinesis (standard forms of occultism).

Upon initially arriving in the Soviet Union to do his research, Vallee, observing hundreds of books on the paranormal on his host's bookshelves, said to him: "We never expected to find such a high level of interest in the paranormal in the Soviet Union." The topics covered by these books ranged from astrology and healing to spiritism and psychic research.[19]

Eugene, the host, responded by saying: "We're ahead of you in the study of the paranormal because the Western churches killed all your witches in the name of their dogma.... You only have yourselves to blame if you have fewer gifted psychics. You've eliminated their genes from the gene pool."[20]

No wonder there have been so many "UFO" encounters in the former Soviet Union!

The Occult Connection with Erich Von Daniken

You might recall my earlier discussion of the theories of the once-wildly-popular Erich Von Daniken and his theories regarding UFOs in the Bible (see Chapter 5). Von Daniken is the writer who said that the ark of the covenant was a radio transmitter used by Moses to communicate with aliens, and that a flying saucer guided the Israelites in the wilderness as a "pillar of fire."

A fact about Von Daniken that is mentioned by very few newspaper reports is that he got his early ideas from the occult in the same way that other UFO advocates received messages from "space brothers." That is, he received paranormal information by means of telepathy from an unknown source as well as from out-of-body experiences.[21] Von Daniken once remarked:

> I know that astronauts visited the earth in ancient time . . . . I was there when the astronauts arrived. Why should anybody believe I am able to leave my body whenever I desire and observe the past, present, and future all at the same time? Nonetheless, it is true. It has been true for many years.[22]

I believe this admission by Von Daniken is significant. There is certainly no one more motivated than Satan and his demons to discredit Christianity by interjecting UFO theology into the Bible. Satan is the real mastermind and inspiration behind the "UFOs-in-the-Bible" theory. And because of Von Daniken's vast literary success, many people have ended up believing not in the miraculous God of the Bible but in aliens with incredible powers.

The Theosophical Backdrop

Anyone who seriously investigates the UFO enigma will soon notice how heavily many UFO groups have borrowed from the Theosophical Society and spiritualism.

Such groups often speak of cosmic masters of wisdom on other planets who psychically communicate through human beings by means of spiritism. Typically messages are received from these cosmic masters while the human being is in a trance state.[23]

The spiritist movement emerged in 1848 at the home of farmer John Fox in Hydesville, New York. It then received a huge shot in the arm from spiritualist Helena Petrovna Blavatsky, the founder of Theosophy, in 1875. Scholar Irving Hexham, commenting on the early UFO books to appear in the 1950s, said that "from the beginning, UFO stories were entangled with religious beliefs of theosophical origin supported by rich occult mythologies."[24] In keeping with this, we read in *The Gods Have Landed: New Religions from Other Worlds:*

> Most nineteenth- and early twentieth-century contact with extraterrestrials occurred in a spiritualist context, more likely than not in a seance. The prime mode of contact was a phenomenon quite familiar to psychic researchers, named "astral travel." A person experiencing astral travel senses his/her body and consciousness separately, and while the body remains in one place, the consciousness travels around.[25]

These are all common themes in the Theosophical Society. The term "Theosophy" literally means "divine wisdom." Among the distinctive New Age ideas taught by Theosophy is the idea that "Ascended Masters" guide humanity's spiritual evolution.

Ascended Masters are thought to be formerly historical persons who have finished their earthly evolutions through reincarnation but are continuing their evolution on a higher plane of existence. Today, even as these Ascended Masters continue in their own evolutions toward the divine, they voluntarily help lesser-evolved human beings to reach the Masters' present level. These Masters give revelations to spiritually attuned human beings.

Though not widely publicized, Theosophy has taught over the years that certain of these "Masters" live on other planets. J. Gordon Melton explains:

> These masters [Blavatsky] termed the Lords of the Flame and the Lord of This World, the head of the hierarchy for humanity. Under these Venusian lords are the Lords of the Seven Rays (or colors) who have direct contact with human adepts such as Blavatsky.[26]

In a very real way, then, the modern UFO movement with its emphasis on contact with aliens through occultic means had its beginnings back in 1875 when Blavatsky founded the Theosophical Society. The parallels between New Age "contactees" and typical occult theosophists are amazing.

Carl Jung and Psychic Experiences

It may surprise some readers to learn that the famous German psychologist Carl Jung (1875–1961) wrote a book about UFOs entitled *Flying Saucers: A Modern Myth of Things Seen in the Sky*. Jung, who himself was involved in the occult, believed that when people saw UFOs they were actually engaged in a psychic experience, since physical evidence always seemed to be lacking for the UFO appearance. In other words, to the person beholding the UFO the experience may seem vividly real, but there is nothing there in a physical sense.[27] Consider Jung's comments:

> There are on record cases where one or more persons see something that physically is not there. For instance, I was once at a spiritualistic seance where four of the five people present saw an object like a moon floating above the abdomen of the medium. They showed me, the fifth person present, exactly where it was, and it was absolutely incomprehensible to them that I could see nothing of the sort.
>
> I know three more cases where certain objects were seen in the clearest detail (in two of them by two persons and in the third by one person) and could afterwards be proved to be nonexistent. Two of these cases happened under my direct observation. Even people who are entirely *compos mentis* [mentally competent] and in full possession of their senses can sometimes see things that do not exist.
>
> I do not know what the explanation is of such happenings . . . . I mention these somewhat remote possibilities because, in such an unusual matter as the UFOs, one has to take every aspect into account.[28]

If there is anything we can learn from Jung's experience, it is this: People who are presently involved in some form of occultism—whether it be clairvoyance, telepathy, out-of-body experiences, astrology, divination, tarot cards, or whatever else—may witness what they believe to be a UFO when in fact nothing is physically there. Because so many people in our country are presently involved in various forms of New Age occultism, perhaps *this* explains why so many in the New Age movement claim to have seen or come into contact with a UFO.

When we keep in mind the scriptural fact that Satan has the ability to bring about counterfeit miracles, signs, and wonders (2 Thessalonians 2:9), I think a viable explanation of those UFO sightings that are not rooted in natural phenomena (see Chapter 4) is that they may in fact be rooted in the work of Satan.

I want to note in closing that God condemns *all* forms of spiritism, channeling, and divination—which are the occultic tools of contact with the alleged "aliens." Deuteronomy 18:10-12 is clear: "Let no one be found among you who . . . practices divination or sorcery, interprets omens, engages in witchcraft, or casts spells, or who is a medium or spiritist or who consults the dead. Anyone who does these things is detestable to the LORD, and because of these detestable practices the LORD your God will drive out those nations before you." Anyone who thus makes contact with "aliens" by means of such occultic tools stands condemned by God.

Having provided this brief general introduction on the connection between occultism and UFO phenomena, we will now investigate the most controversial aspect of UFO studies: *the abduction experience*. We will see that there is a very strong connection between occultism and abductions.

9

"Alien" Abductions: Terror from the Sky

A lien abductions have become a phenomena to be reckoned with in Western society. Presently there are books, magazines, videos, conferences, societies, 900-numbers, film festivals, and support groups for victims of alien abduction.[1] A quick look at the bestseller lists over the last decade reveals that books published on the abduction experience have outnumbered (in terms of sales) books on all other subjects related to UFOs combined.[2]

The alien-abduction phenomenon seems to have exploded in 1966 with the case of Betty and Barney Hill. According to their testimony, they had gotten lost one night driving through the mountains. Years later they read some literature on UFOs, spent some time with some psychiatrists, and, under hypnosis, suddenly "remembered" having been kidnapped by aliens the night they got lost. While under hypnosis they "remembered" having been subjected to a variety of indignities.

Since the Hill incident, there have been numerous books, movies, and TV docudramas dealing with this couple's strange experience. With the Hills, the abduction experience penetrated Western culture and became a topic of fascination.[3]

The abduction phenomenon has now snowballed. There are people all across the country who have "discovered," under hypnosis, that they too have been abducted by aliens. One poll made the wild claim that nearly 3 percent of Americans have been abducted by aliens.[4] (To put that statistic into perspective, if you're in an auditorium seating 1000 adults, 30 of them have likely been abducted by aliens.)

The Typical Abduction Experience

People who claim to have been abducted typically report being taken from a room against their will and then being floated upward into an alien spacecraft, where they are laid on an examining table. While in the spacecraft, the abductees are poked, prodded, and often molested in a sexual manner. Sometimes the aliens will induce rapid, intense sexual arousal and even orgasm.

Painful medical procedures are often performed by groups of aliens. Instruments are used to penetrate virtually every part of the abductee's body, including the nose, sinuses, eyes, ears, arms, legs, feet, abdomen, genitalia, and, more rarely, the chest. Sometimes people are dismembered. Body parts and organs are severed from the body, only to be reattached later.[5] Some report an object being inserted deep into the nose.

Part of the examination involves the alien examiner pressing on the abductee's vertebrae one by one, from the top of the spine to the coccyx. Another part of the examination involves the aliens using their fingers to "dance" over their captives for some unknown reason. One abductee reports that it felt like the alien was playing piano on her body. Another abductee reported it felt as if the alien were "typewriting" on her.[6]

Some abductees report that following this physical trauma they are subjected to some sort of spiritual examination, with their souls being probed and their memories being examined in some way. This has become known among some in the UFO community as "Mindscan."

> During Mindscan, the abductee is still on the table; the being bends over him or her, comes so close their foreheads might touch. The being then looks deeply, penetratingly into the abductee's eyes .... Abductees commonly sense some sort of information is being extracted from their minds.[7]

Abductees are then given messages in their minds that they take back with them as they return to normal life.[8]

> Often these messages concern the purpose of the alien's visit—to interbreed with humanity in order to produce a new hybrid race. Abductees are told that they themselves, or humanity as a whole, are somehow creations of the aliens. The messages can be eschatological in character, forecasting a coming catastrophe or the dawning of a New Age.[9]

Sometimes female abductees are told that they are being impregnated with alien seed. Later, after they have allegedly been pregnant for a time, they are reabducted and the hybrid fetus is allegedly removed, and the woman is no longer pregnant.[10]

Abductees typically reported that they were powerless to prevent what was happening to them. The moment they were returned home, they forgot everything—or nearly everything—that had occurred. Only under hypnosis were they able to "remember" what had happened.

It would seem, for the most part, that only younger people are abducted by aliens. If you're over 30 years old, you can relax, because you probably won't be abducted, the experts tell us:

> The good news, if you are over thirty, is that if you have not been abducted by now, it's not likely to happen. The aliens are said to focus on younger people, with abductions often beginning in childhood. The bad news is that you may already have been abducted but just cannot remember. The aliens, it is believed, tend to "mask" memories of abductions. It is only recently that these memories have begun to surface in significant numbers. Often the stories emerge painfully in therapy sessions . . . using hypnotic regression techniques. The aliens, it is claimed, have abducted hundreds of thousands of people.[11]

The aliens involved in abduction experiences come in a variety of shapes and sizes. But most—at least in regard to those reported in the United States—resemble those portrayed in Steven Spielberg's movie *Close Encounters of the Third Kind.* They may be characterized as follows:

- 3½ to 4½ feet tall
- About 40 pounds
- Large head, equal in proportion to a five-month human fetus
- Heavy brow ridge
- Round eyes without pupils, large and "Oriental" looking
- Apertures rather than ears
- Small, indistinct nose
- Small, slitlike mouth without lips
- Slender torso and long, thin arms
- Skin grayish and elastic, reptilelike.[12]

I think a rather important aspect of the typical abduction experience is the dreamlike state in which it is often said to take place. Researcher John Whitmore reports that "in many of the cases in which the abduction is at least partially recalled prior to the use of hypnosis, it is recalled *as a dream* rather than as an objective event."[13] Whitmore further notes:

> Often the abductee reports being outside her body during certain stages of the event, or views herself in the third person throughout. Abductees report very common dream imagery during the course of their ordeals, such as floating or flying, falling endlessly, or appearing naked in a public place. Time and space appear disjointed in a nonsensical, dreamlike way. Day instantly becomes night, the inside of a room or craft appears far larger than its exterior dimensions would allow, and events which subjectively seem to have taken hours are found to have taken minutes, or vice versa.[14]

The reason I view this as important relates to what I will talk about in the next section—the occult connection. The fact is that in various cults and world religions, Satan and the powers of darkness often seek to work through mystical experiences. And the dreamlike state described above fits right in with the typical mystical experiences that people in various cultic groups have had.

The apostle Paul tells us that Satan as the god of this age *blinds* the minds of unbelievers (2 Corinthians 4:4). Moreover, we are told that Satan has the power to bring about "counterfeit miracles, signs and wonders" (2 Thessalonians 2:9). Could it be that, particularly for those already involved in the occult, Satan blinds their minds and in some way induces a mystical dreamlike experience in their minds in which they "perceive" that they are being abducted (though they are not actually *physically* abducted)—a dream that is later "recalled" and "remembered" by means of hypnosis as being a "true event"?

This is certainly in keeping with the earlier-noted observations of Carl Jung, who himself was involved in the occult. As noted in Chapter 8, Jung was attending a spiritistic seance, and four of the five people there "saw" phenomena while Jung, an observer, did not. The four people even pointed to the object they saw, but Jung could not perceive it.[15] This would seem to indicate that people who are deeply involved in some form of occultism may witness what they believe to be physical phenomena when in fact nothing is physically there. Certainly if there was a satanically induced dream-state in a person involved in the occult, that person might perceive certain things as real ("aliens") when in fact they are not real.

Of course, it may also be that in these mystical states, demons are actually mimicking aliens in order to deceive the abductees. Just as Satan can mimic an angel of light (2 Corinthians 11:14), so demons have the capacity *and the motivation* to mimic alien entities *if the result* will be the instilling of a worldview in the abductees that is contrary to Christianity— a worldview that will subsequently be communicated to the masses in bestselling books and television talk shows. The strategy—if this is in fact what is happening—is a malevolent stroke of genius. Perhaps the feasibility of such a scenario will become more convincing to you as you consider what follows—the connection between alien abductions and occultism.

The Occult Connection

As we noted in the previous chapter, there is a very strong connection between UFO phenomena in general and occultism. The same is true in a more specific sense in regard to alleged alien abductions. This connection has been noted by numerous experts in the field.

For example, at a UFO-and-abduction conference held at the prestigious Massachusetts Institute of Technology (MIT), Keith Basterfield, a research officer for UFO Research Australia, focused attention on the correlation between UFO events (including abductions) and paranormal phenomena such as poltergeists (noisy-ghost phenomena), apparitions, and psychic healing.[16] Speaking of cases he personally examined, he pointed to the "incredible history of psychic phenomena which might explain why they were abducted."[17]

Researchers have noted that while abductions seem common to people involved in Eastern religions (Hinduism and Zen Buddhism, for example), they don't seem to happen among evangelical Christians.[18] For example, Mary, who claims to have been abducted by aliens, talks about how in her earlier participation in Zen Buddhism there was the practice of "identifying with deities" and expressing "compassion and understanding toward disembodied spirits." She spoke of how contact with the various beings "is not a new human experience. It's just in a different frame of reference . . . ."[19] Her participation in Zen Buddhism no doubt paved the way for her later abduction experience.

How different it is for Christians! Indeed, alien abductions are simply not occurring in the Judeo-Christian tradition. We are told by one non-Christian researcher that "Jews and Christians have become such stick-in-the-muds [in regard to UFO experiences] compared to Eastern religions, such as Tibetan Buddhism, which have always recognized a vast range of spirit entities in the cosmos . . . ."[20]

A key means of demonstrating the connection between alien abductions and occultism is to examine the *spiritual effect* which the abductions have on people. Researchers have long noted that people who claim to have been abducted say that their perception of themselves, the world, and their place in it has profoundly changed as a result of the abduction experience.[21]

> Their religious views are more syncretic, finding in all religions some form of spiritual truth. Many abductees report paranormal talents gained as a result of their experience. The ability to cause electromagnetic disturbances, to travel out of body, or to read minds is often claimed. This pattern of personality change is quite similar to that found among people who report near-death experiences, another phenomenon with heavy religious overtones. These experiences, however subjective they may be, have powerful and long-lasting effects upon the psyche of the individual, prompting permanent changes in worldview and lifestyle.[22]

Some abductees develop "strong psychic abilities, including clairvoyance or the ability to perceive at a distance."[23] One abductee I read about felt it necessary to start meeting with a shamanic (Native American Indian) healer following his experience.[24] Another abductee felt led to explore Tibetan Buddhism and read books by Carlos Castaneda, an occultist, in an effort to more fully understand his experience.[25]

Still another abductee said, "I feel I shed some of my old beliefs." She said she no longer "blindly" follows "someone else or some organization." As a Catholic, she had been raised to feel that she was "being disobedient to God" when she followed "my own instincts" or asked questions that challenged Church belief.[26] As a result of her abduction experience, she no longer feels that way.

Not only that, but many abductees come to adopt a New Age worldview that recognizes the oneness of all things in the universe:

Abductees come to appreciate that the universe is filled with intelligences and is itself intelligent. They develop a sense of awe before a mysterious cosmos that becomes sacred and ensouled. The sense of separation from all the rest of creation breaks down and the experience of oneness becomes an essential aspect of the evolution of the abductees' consciousness . . . . As their experiences are brought into full consciousness, abductees seem to feel increasingly a sense of oneness with all beings and all of creation. This is often expressed through a special love of nature and a deep connection with animals and animal spirits.[27]

All this should give the discerning reader a clue as to the true origin of alien abduction experiences. If only those people who are already involved in the occult are having these abduction experiences, and if these experiences lead to the development of further occult powers, and if a person develops a New Age worldview as a result of the experience, does it not seem clear that Satan and his demonic spirits are behind it all? This conclusion becomes even more probable in view of what follows.

The Strong Resemblance to Shamanism

An important evidence that demonstrates the connection between alien abductions and occultism relates to shamanism.[28] Shamanism is a religion that focuses on the unseen world; shamans are occultic priests or priestesses who use magic and divination to cure the sick and control events. Of great relevance to our study is the fact that in a shamanistic initiation ceremony, there are visionary experiences that are strikingly parallel to what UFO abductees go through.

During a shamanic initiation ceremony, which is rooted in occultism, the candidate is in an entranced state, and his soul leaves the body and he is taken into an underworld. While he is there, demonic beings capture the candidate, tear him apart, and then reassemble him. Following this reassembly the person has new knowledge and new seemingly magical powers. Typically a rock crystal is allegedly inserted deep into the candidate's head, which is said to give him power. Further examination of the initiate takes place by these demonic entities in the midst of a uniform but sourceless light. When the initiate returns, he may have been unconscious for hours or days. The person then leads a changed life, and has new magical powers as well as the ability to communicate with the spirit world.[29]

Can you see the strong parallels between this occultic ceremony and alien abductions? Consider the key factors:

- A mystical experience
- A lapse of time
- A forceful examination
- Being torn apart and put back together again
- Implantation of an object into the head
- New powers and ability to communicate with the spirit world following the experience[30]

Just as shamanism is rooted in the occult, where Satan reigns supreme, so I believe that these abduction experiences are rooted in the occult. The similarities between these two types of experience are just too close to ignore.

The Strong Resemblance to Fairy Folklore

In the book *The Gods Have Landed: New Religions from Other Worlds,* we are told that many scholars outside the field of religious studies have noted the similarities between abduction experiences and fairy folklore.[31] According to fairy legend, fairies very much enjoyed abducting human beings and causing their victims to experience periods of "missing time" similar to those reported by abductees.

It was believed in times past that fairies could not properly reproduce, and for this reason needed the aid of human beings to sustain their species. "Encounters with them were often erotic experiences for the humans involved, and sometimes led to a continuing series of contacts resembling the repeat abductions seen in modern stories."[32]

Related to such fairy legends, in 1990 Dr. Jacques Vallee wrote a book entitled *Confrontations: A Scientist's Search for Alien Contact* in which he examined over 100 UFO incidents around the world.[33] In it he pointed to the diabolical nature of the visitors. He said their "'scientific' experiments [on abductees] are crude to the point of being grotesque. The 'medical examination' to which abductees are said to be subjected, often accompanied by sadistic sexual manipulation, is reminiscent of the medieval tales of encounters with demons."[34]

Vallee also pointed out that the existence of creatures who fly through the air and steal humans for sexual purposes is a belief by no means confined to Western culture and UFOs. He notes similar folklore among Native Americans of Mexico and South America.[35]

A Harvard Psychiatrist Becomes a UFO Believer

Perhaps the most important UFO convert in recent days is Pulitzer Prize winner and Harvard Medical School psychiatrist, John Mack. He is the author of the controversial book *Abduction: Human Encounters with Aliens,* in which he documents 13 of his case studies on individuals who claim to have been abducted by aliens. (This hot book was featured on *Oprah, 48 Hours, Dateline, Newsweek, Time,* and *The New York Times Magazine.*) Mack is firmly convinced of the veracity of the abductees' claims. As we will see below, however, Mack's book provides further evidence for the connection between abduction experiences and occultism.

One of Mack's admitted goals is to convince skeptical readers that extraterrestrial life-forms are real and have visited planet Earth. Mack says he himself was once a skeptic. "The idea that there could be some kind of alien beings taking people from their homes and doing things to them was totally preposterous," he recalls thinking at the time.[36] But the more research he did, the more he became convinced that alien abductions have taken place.[37]

People have sat up and taken notice of Mack's claims because of his prestigious position. "Ordinarily," Oprah Winfrey declared, "we would not even put people on television—on our show certainly—who make such bizarre claims . . . . But we were intrigued by this man . . . . Dr. Mack is a respected professor who teaches at Harvard University. He is an eminent psychiatrist."[38] He has a medical degree. He is a psychiatrist. He teaches at Harvard. And he won a Pulitzer Prize. People therefore listen to him.

Mack is careful to state that he is not "presuming that everything [the abductees] say is literally true." Nevertheless, he writes of his "growing conviction about the authenticity of these reports . . . . No plausible alternative explanation . . . has been discovered."[39]

Mack bases his conclusions in *Abduction* on over 3½ years of work with more than 100 "experiencers" (UFO parlance for "abductees"). In each case, the recollections of the experiencers were a combination of conscious recall and memories that surfaced through hypnosis. Mack speaks of the sincerity and genuineness of the experiencers:

> What I say is that these are people who as best as I can tell have no reason to be distorting this

phenomenon, who have nothing to gain personally, who have come forward reluctantly, who do
not remotely demonstrate a form of mental dis-
turbance that could account for what they're saying and who, with or without hypnosis and with
intense feeling, describe what [sounds like] real
experience . . . . So I say these people are speaking authentically, genuinely, and that it's a mystery
I can't explain.[40]

Mack first became interested in the abduction phenomenon after being introduced to Budd Hopkins, considered by
many observers to be the father of the abduction-awareness
movement. They met in 1990, and Hopkins told Mack about
people from all parts of the country who had had abduction
experiences. Just a month later, Mack met with four of the abductees and was fascinated by what they said. Their stories, if
true, had profound implications for beliefs about philosophy,
spirituality, and society in general.

One of the more disturbing implications that Mack deals
with is the "apparently faulty view" that human beings are really in control of things:

We like to believe we are in control of our world,
that we can bulldoze it, blow up the enemy. That
illusion of control is deeply built into the Western
psyche. This [abduction] phenomenon strikes at
the core of that and says not only are we *not* in
control, that some kind of intelligence can break
through and do threatening things to people for
which there's no defense, it also shatters another
belief—that we are the preeminent intelligence, if
not the only intelligence, in the cosmos. It makes
a mockery of our arrogance.[41]

One thing that profoundly impacted Mack's attitude toward the abduction phenomenon was the utter intensity of the abductee's experiences. During hypnosis sessions, abductees "will literally scream with terror and their whole body shakes."[42] Mack says there is nothing, clinically, that could produce that kind of response "except the reliving of something that has been done to them. There is no other condition I know of that can elicit or bring forth that kind of emotional expression. Then that leaves me with the question, 'What was it that was done?' "[43]

In my view, all the people Mack interviewed *did* in fact have an intense experience of some kind. But it was not with aliens; instead, it was with demonic spirits. I believe that either the powers of darkness induced a powerful mystical experience in the brains of these individuals, or else demonic spirits took on some kind of appearance, mimicking aliens from outer space. The powers of darkness are responsible for the sheer terror these people encountered. This hypothesis receives support not only from the fact that Mack himself is open to the occult, but from the fact that many of the abductees he reports on were involved in the occult as well.

Mack's Openness to Occultism

In examining Mack's background, it becomes very clear that he has been open to certain forms of occultism in the past. In fact, in the 1970s Mack was very open to occultist Carlos Casteneda, Werner Erhard's est, and Esalen.[44] Mack also concedes that he is a firm believer in auras—energy fields around us that some New Age and occultic "sensitives" claim to be able to see.[45]

Est and Esalen are Human Potential seminars that basically teach attendees that "your are your own god" and "you can create your own reality." The seminars are heavily influenced by Eastern mysticism and promise enlightenment regarding one's true potential. These seminars typically seek to induce an altered state of consciousness in attendees to lead them to question their former understanding of reality. Such mystical experiences cause attendees to seek a new understanding of reality—such as the New Age worldview—that can explain their mystical experience. If Mack participated in these seminars, as he claims, then the groundwork was laid for his openness to the mystical abduction experiences he would write about years later.

Carlos Casteneda was a popular occultist who wrote books about his adventures with Don Juan. These books sold millions of copies and served to make American Indian sorcery palatable to modern tastes. His works have served for many people as a direct inroad into modern shamanism (which, as we noted earlier, involves mystical ceremonies with marked parallels to the abduction experience). Hence, with Mack's fondness for the works of Casteneda, he was certainly prepared in a major way to become an advocate of the similar abduction experience.

Abductees Mack Reports On

A number of the abduction cases Mack reports on in his book clearly involve occultism. One abductee held to a New Age concept of God, saying He was merely a "source of energy."[46] This view of God is rooted in an occultic worldview which, I believe, opened this person up to demonic affliction that typically accompanies occultism. *These demons mimicked aliens.*

Another abductee Mack reports on admits that from the time he was a teenager he had participated in such things as mind-body (New Age) healing workshops and different forms of Eastern meditation, and that he was a member of a spiritistic church.[47] Now recall what we said about spiritism in the previous chapter: There is a direct connection between spiritism (contact with paranormal spirit entities) and so-called alien contact (that is, contact with aliens by means of channel-ing, which is just a modern form of spiritism). This person's in-volvement with occultic spiritism no doubt paved the way for his abduction experience years later.

Still another abductee Mack reports on says that from a very young age she had a great interest in reading books—especially books about ghosts and poltergeists (noisy spirits). She went to church with her family almost every Sunday, but either dismissed or reinterpreted key Christian doctrines. For example, she didn't like the idea of "original sin." So that doc-trine wasn't a part of her belief system. She did, however, like the Holy Spirit, whom she describes as a "connective tissue that binds all of reality together."[48] This is a New Age reinter-pretation of the Holy Spirit (a key New Age doctrine is monism—the idea that "all is one").

By the time this person was 11 or 12 years of age, she was struggling with the dichotomy of good and evil, and was subsequently drawn to reading about other religions. When she became an undergraduate in college, she began participat-ing in studies of extrasensory perception (ESP). Sometime after this she had an out-of-body experience. "I felt like I got out of my body and I couldn't get back in, and I was gone for about two days."[49]

Again, I believe that this person's rejection of Christian-ity and her participation in different forms of occultism—such as out-of-body experiences—paved the way for an abduction experience later in life. But as I noted earlier, these were not real aliens; they were simply demonic spirits influencing her. These demons either induced a mystical experience in her mind or else took on some kind of an appearance and mim-icked alien entities.

Still another abductee Mack reports on was involved in karate training in his earlier years. He spoke about how he sought to control the *chi* energy as a part of his training.[50] It is critical to understand this chi energy and its worldview (Tao-ism) as a backdrop to seeing how this opened the door to an eventual abduction experience.

The word "Taoism" refers to a Chinese philosophy based on the teachings of Lao Tzu (sixth to fourth century B.C.) and Chuang Tzu (about 399–295 B.C.). The central theme of Tao-ism has to do with harmony with the "natural flow" of the universe. Letting nature take its course is believed to be the key to happiness and fulfillment. Taoists therefore say that life should be approached with the goal of "taking no action that is contrary to Nature."[51]

To Taoists, nature is synonymous with the Tao, which makes up the entire universe; it is elusive, hidden, mysterious.[52] The Tao, in turn, is divided into two forces called *yin* and *yang*. Yin and yang represent the negative and positive aspects of the universe, each flowing into the other in a continuous cycle of change.

> *Yin* is characterized as the negative force of darkness, coldness, and emptiness. *Yang* stands for the positive energy that produces light, warmth, and fullness. These alternating forces are indestructible and inexhaustible. They contradict as well as complement each other.[53]

Taoist philosophy sees the universe as a balance between these two inseparable, opposing forces. All manifestations of the Tao—and all changes in nature—are believed to be generated by the dynamic interplay of these two polar forces.

Blending with the course of nature, or becoming one with the Tao, was the common goal among Taoists. Both the *Lao Tzu* and *Chuang Tzu,* the oldest primary works of Taoism, set forth the notion that meditation, along with breathing exercises, greatly aids those attempting to become one with the Tao.[54]

In time various Chinese shamans and magicians incorporated into their own existing belief systems the ideas of Taoism, producing what came to be known as *religious* Taoism. The primary objective of religious Taoists was the attainment of physical immortality. Meditation, along with various magical practices, physical exercises, breathing exercises, and sexual practices, was considered the means of retaining vigor and achieving everlasting life.[55]

The practice of breath control (called *chi kung*), in particular, figured prominently not only in the quest for immortality but for control of the universe. Chi (sometimes written as *qi* or *ki*) was believed to be a mystical energy, a "substance surrounding and including all things, which brought even distant points into direct physical contact." Chi is understood to be the energy and matter produced by the interaction between yin and yang. "Since one single substance joined all corners of the cosmos into a single organic unity, it followed that mastery of qi was equivalent to mastery of the universe."[56]

Religious Taoists believed that breath control is the means of tapping into and controlling the chi force:

> The Taoist believed that, through his own supremely concentrated breath control, he could inhale the Chi of the universe into his body and fuse it with his own self-energized Chi. This combination could only result in a healthful extension of life. This practice demands extraordinary patience and consistently deep meditation. The practitioner, after clearing his mind of extraneous thoughts in a kind of "fast of the mind," must focus only on the constant feeling and sound of the inhalation and exhalation of his respiration. This experience will enable one, in time, to circulate and direct the power of Chi into any part of the body.[57]

Mack's abductee patient sought to use the mind to become one with the "One" and manipulate this mystical energy within the body. He sought to control the chi force.[58] And, as I have demonstrated, the whole emphasis on chi is derived from a monistic, occultic worldview. Combining this with the fact that this patient was also involved in Native American shamanism,[59] it seems clear that the occult door was wide open for a later abduction experience in this person's life.

I could go on and on, but I think you're beginning to see my point. There is an extremely strong connection between those who claim to have been abducted by aliens and a former involvement in some form of the occult. Whether it's Native American shamanism, out-of-body experiences, divination, spiritism, or clairvoyance, these and other forms of occultism are a doorway straight into "alien abductions"—which are, in reality, demonic intrusions of the human mind.

In a later chapter, I will drive this point home even more forcefully as we examine "demonized delusions in the end times." Before I close this chapter, however, I want to briefly touch on the problem of using hypnotism as a basis upon which to "reconstruct" memories.

The Problem with Hypnosis

Abductees typically recall little or anything on a conscious level about the abduction experience. But certain telltale signs—unaccounted-for loss of time, or the sense of a presence in the bedroom before falling asleep—tip off the counselor regarding the possibility of an abduction. Hypnosis is then used to "fill in the holes."

Mack and other psychiatrists around the country have often used hypnosis as a means of helping patients "remember" something that occurred in the past. Sometimes Mack's patients weep and shout with agony and terror as they "recover buried memories" of alien encounters.[60] It is a rude awakening to suddenly "discover" that since childhood you have been abducted by sinister aliens who have used you as a guinea pig in an intergalactic hybrid-breeding program and that you have had probes inserted up your nose and have had your private parts examined time and time again by reptilian perverts.

The question that has often been raised is, Do abduction therapists somehow "lead" their patients into giving—consciously or otherwise—the kinds of answers that patients think their therapists want to hear?[61] Mack concedes the possibility that this can happen in certain counseling sessions, but not in *his* counseling sessions.[62] "I do not lead people. We look *together* at a shared mystery, but they are not alone in the strange, reality-shattering matter here."[63]

Experts note that hypnosis is all about suggestion. And, as one critic put it, "for every genuine buried memory unearthed by hypnotists, many more false memories have been implanted."[64] Some critics have charged that this may be the case in regard to some of Mack's patients. In fact, one critic noted that *Time* magazine "quoted one of Mack's subjects as saying that she was given UFO literature to read in preparation for her sessions and was asked obvious leading questions."[65]

Hypnotist Michael Yapko, author of the textbook *Trancework*, says that the great strength of hypnosis is that under trance "you can accept and respond to a suggested reality. Therapists like Mack may be oblivious to the fact that they're creating the experiences they then have to treat. These phenomena are not arising independent of his influence."[66]

As we read in the book *Close Encounters of the Fourth Kind: Alien Abduction, UFOs, and the Conference at MIT,* any revelatory statements that surface during a hypnosis session "speak of the subject's susceptibility and suggestibility, role playing, following the lead of the hypnotist." Indeed, "the subject is likely to confabulate fiction that is true, untrue, or partly true. Details may come out, but the witness cannot distinguish between truth and falsehood. Experts are unanimous in their discrediting of any hypnosis-based reality of what happened."[67]

Furthermore, in 1985 the American Medical Association's Council on Scientific Affairs warned that "recollections obtained during hypnosis not only fail to be more accurate but actually appear to be generally less reliable than recall."[68] In view of this fact alone, it seems foolish to build an entire theory based on a series of subjective hypnotic sessions.

The *Encyclopaedia Britannica* states that the central phenomenon in hypnosis is "suggestibility—a state of greatly enhanced receptiveness and responsiveness to suggestions and stimuli."[69] Hence, as Christian researcher Vishal Mangalwadi points out—

> the process that takes place under hypnosis is not pure "recall" of previous memories, but "confabulation"—an attempt by the subject to please the hypnotist. The subject fills the gaps in memory with unrelated memories, fantasies, and fabrications. The very questions that a hypnotist asks become suggestions, prompting subjects to fabricate memories.[70]

UFO critic Philip Klass has concluded that hypnosis makes it possible to derive "memories" of things which have never happened.[71] The scholarly book *The Gods Have Landed: New Religions from Other Worlds* agrees, noting that "it would be premature . . . to dismiss the possibility that many, if not all, abduction memories are confabulations of the subconscious, guided by the preconceptions of the hypnotist."[72]

It seems clear, then, that hypnosis as a diagnostic tool and aid to memory is simply "faulty equipment" that yields unreliable results. But I would offer a further very important observation.

During hypnotic sessions, the counselee is in a mystical altered state of consciousness in which the rational mind recedes. Christian researchers of occult phenomena have often noted that while in *any* kind of altered state of consciousness, the person may become prey to demonic influences.

Is it possible, then, that during this mystical, dreamlike hypnotic state—under the influence of powerful demonic spirits who work "counterfeit miracles, signs and wonders" (2 Thessalonians 2:9)—the person suddenly "perceives" certain things as real ("aliens") when in fact they are not real at all? Is this particularly a possibility for counselees who have had previous involvement in the occult? Such a conclusion cannot be easily dismissed in view of the evidence.

——— 10 ———

The Strange Case of Whitley Strieber

hitley Strieber is a professional writer who in his earlier years was an author of horror fiction. One of his commercially successful and critically acclaimed books was entitled *The Wolfen*. This book featured gray creatures who, in Strieber's description, "hid in the cracks of life, and used their immense intelligence to hunt down beings as their natural and proper prey."[1] He then coauthored a few nonfiction books that didn't sell well, and his career was at a crossroads. He was in the throes of writing other books when his life suddenly took a turn for the worse: *Alien visitations began.*

Strieber says that before the visitations began, he didn't believe in UFOs. He wants people to be clear that he is not some kind of a fringe "nut case" who is predisposed to this sort of thing.

> I did not believe in UFOs at all before this happened. And I would have laughed in the face of anybody who claimed contact. Period. I am not a candidate for conversion to any new religion that involves belief in benevolent space brothers, or in unidentified flying objects as the craft of intergalactic saints—or sinners.[2]

Nevertheless, the visitations came. Here is how it happened.

It was toward the end of 1985. After Christmas that year, Strieber found himself sinking into a deep depression—so deep that he couldn't write anymore.

He was with his wife, Anne, and his young son, Andrew, at their family log cabin in upstate New York. For no apparent reason, Strieber began lashing out at his family and friends. He became verbally abusive to them. He also found himself becoming confused by simple events. Worst of all, he began sensing that "strange people" were hiding in their cabin at night. He became so paranoid and phobic about this that he would secretly go around at night and check all the closets and look under the beds before retiring for the night. He also kept a shotgun nearby.

Strieber wasn't just deteriorating mentally; he was suffering physically as well. For some strange reason, he had developed an unexplainable infection in the forefinger of his right hand. He had also developed some rather severe rectal pain. Combined with this was an overall sense of fatigue that alternated with flulike symptoms that wouldn't go away. He was in bad shape. And things were getting worse.

Psychologically Strieber continued to plummet to new lows. He felt he was being watched all the time. The paranoia continued to grow to the point that he felt constantly on guard against an unknown threat. Anne became so disturbed at Whitley's behavior that she contemplated divorcing him. Whitley was going from bad to worse, and she had had about all she could stand.

The Breakthrough

Then, on January 3, 1986, a breakthrough emerged. Somehow, the cause of Whitley's psychological and physical suffering surfaced in his consciousness. "The confused swirl resolved into a specific series of recollections, and when I saw what they were, I just about exploded with terror and utter disbelief."[3]

Strieber suddenly "remembered" being abducted in the middle of the night from his bedroom. Small, horrifying alien creatures crept up to his bedside, and by their mental powers they controlled him and paralyzed him. They promptly took him out of the cabin naked, and levitated him to some kind of an examination theater in the sky from some spot in the snowy woods.

Once Strieber was in the small, roundish theater, he felt much like an animal in a laboratory experiment. He was helpless. He was nude. He felt like a monkey strapped to a table with all kinds of electrodes attached to his body.

Strieber reports that he was subjected to a series of gruesome experiments and operations by alien creatures. The aliens—insectlike creatures with almond-shaped eyes—allegedly implanted something into his brain through one of his nostrils and inserted another object up his rectum.[4] "They inserted this thing into my rectum. It seemed to swarm into me as if it had a life of its own. Apparently its purpose was to take samples, possibly of fecal matter, but at the time I had the impression that I was being raped, and . . . I felt anger."[5] This was a horrendous experience.

Strieber claims he felt helpless and uncomfortable in the aliens' presence, and he felt violated.[6] Some of the experiences he suffered with the aliens were sexual in nature.[7] The aliens left him feeling frightened, depressed, suffering from nightmares, and fearing for his family's safety (his wife and son).[8]

There were apparently different kinds of alien creatures. Some of the aliens were small, three-foot-tall robotlike beings. These smallest aliens moved with rapid, ugly mechanical movements as they sped around him. There were also some elongated, delicate, spindly, leather-skinned five-foot-tall aliens. And then there were the taller, more slender aliens that had "prominent and mesmerizing black eyes." The eyes of these creatures seemed like black abysses. They had a very insectlike quality about them.

Strieber recalls that as he was examined, one of the five-foot-tall aliens in particular observed him with careful scrutiny. "She had those amazing, electrifying eyes . . . the huge, staring eyes of the old gods . . . . They were featureless, in the sense that I could see neither pupil nor iris."[9] This alien seemingly looked straight into Strieber's soul with a relentless, penetrating gaze. "It was as if every vulnerable detail of my self were known to this being . . . . I could actually feel the presence of that other person within me—which was as disturbing as it was curiously sensual."[10]

He later reflected that this alien had an uncanny resemblance to the ancient goddess Ishtar. "Paint her eyes entirely black, remove her hair, and there is my image as it hangs before me now in my mind's eye, the ancient and terrible one, the bringer of wisdom, the ruthless questioner."[11]

Strieber's fear at what he encountered was overwhelming and pervasive. "What was left was a body in a state of raw fear so great that it swept about me like a thick, suffocating curtain, turning paralysis into a condition that seemed close to death."[12]

The book *Communion* chronicles Strieber's abductions by these hideous aliens. He talks about how the aliens came to him during the middle of the night, and how their visits were often accompanied by weird lights in the sky. The insectlike aliens would appear uninvited and unannounced—often accompanied by strange rapping sounds. They occasionally punished him if he wasn't living the way they desired. Looking back, Strieber now refers to the visitors as "soul eaters" and "predators." "Mostly they terrified me," Strieber said. "One does not want to develop a relationship with a hungry panther."[13]

Communion is one of the bestselling UFO books ever published. It shot to the top of the *New York Times* bestseller list and stayed there for almost a full year. The book was later made into a movie starring Christopher Walken (playing the role of Whitley Strieber).[14]

Sometime later, Strieber came out with a sequel entitled *Transformation*. Because of the public interest in these two books, Strieber appeared on such television shows as *Good Morning America, The Phil Donohue Show*, and *The Tonight Show* with Johnny Carson.[15] Obviously, these books have played a tremendous role in the resurgence of interest in UFOs in America.[16]

Whitley Strieber and the Occult

There is no question that Strieber has suffered through a horrendous experience. The question is, Did Strieber come into contact with genuine aliens from outer space? Was Strieber abducted by extraterrestrials from another galaxy? I don't think so.

I have already discussed in considerable detail how people who claim to have been abducted by aliens typically have a history of occultic involvement. Whitley Strieber fits this profile.

As a backdrop, I should mention that Strieber has a Catholic background. According to his own testimony, however, he ended up having severe doubts about the Catholic church and its teachings:

> I was deeply conflicted about my Catholicism, wondering whether the tenets of my faith could be fitted to the picture I was forming of the world. I asked why the pope hadn't saved the Jews from Hitler. I asked why the Church had burned people at the stake, and what on earth did abstaining from

meat on Friday have to do with getting to heaven? And if the worst punishment in hell was to get a glimpse of heaven and not get to go, then what about the nuns in Limbo who were there caring for the unbaptized babies the angels didn't want to bother with? They'd had more than a glimpse of heaven. They'd been there for a while. So wasn't sending them to Limbo actually sending them to the depths of a personal hell?[17]

Besides rejecting his Catholic roots, Strieber had also been quite open to occultism in his past. To begin with, Strieber had been involved for 15 years in the teachings of mystic occultist G. I. Gurdjieff and of P. D. Ouspensky.

I spent fifteen years involved with the Gurdjieff Foundation, primarily because so much of the thought of G. I. Gurdjieff and his disciple P. D. Ouspensky involved the triad as a primary expression of the essential structure of life, and I have always been fascinated with the significance of this figure.[18]

George Ivanovitch Gurdjieff (1872–1949) had been introduced to occultism by his father, and he retained a profound interest in occultism for the rest of his life. He developed what is best described as a form of esoteric Christianity—blending in elements of the occult, mysticism, Zen, witchcraft, shamanism, existentialism, and psychology. Gurdjieff's disciple, Peter Demianovich Ouspensky, popularized his teachings to the point where followers met in groups called "G-O" (G for Gurdjieff and O for Ouspensky). This mystical, occultic belief system no doubt contributed to Strieber's abduction experience.

Strieber also experimented with paganism.[19] He once commented, "I have experimented with worshipping the earth as a goddess/mother."[20] He also expressed openness to ancient nature religions and shamanism.[21] (Recall from the previous chapter that shamanistic initiation ceremonies hold a number of parallels with the typical abduction experience.) In the following extended quotation, Strieber tells us all about his participation in a Wiccan ceremony and his openness to shamanism:

> I was in a small town near Madison, Wisconsin, having a very unusual experience along with Dora Ruffner and Selena Fox, a leader of Circle Sanctuary, as witnesses and participants.
>
> Circle is the primary networking organization of the Wiccan religion. Wicca is also known as Witchcraft, but it has no relationship to Satanism and other such perversions. It is recognized by the United States government as a legitimate religion, and many of its ministers, such as Ms. Fox, can perform marriages and carry out all the other legally recognized functions of the clergy. Dora and Anne and I were interested in Wicca because, when all the superstitious nonsense that surrounds it is cleared away, it emerges as an ancient Western expression of shamanism, which is the oldest of all human religious traditions. In this it is very similar to Native American and African religions . . . .
>
> Sunday night was windy and moonlit. Selena, Dora, and I went out through a meadow of chest-high grass and flowers, up the side of a hill to Selena's ceremonial stone circle, which is located in a grove of ancient oaks. The wind was

tossing the trees, making wild blue shadows on the ground. It was a beautiful moment.

The three of us entered the circle and stood facing one another at its center. Selena was about to begin the ceremony when we heard the footsteps of a fourth person approaching. These footsteps came close to the north point of the circle and stopped for a moment. I was disturbed, because they came right into a patch of moonlight and I couldn't see anyone. Assuming that it must be another person, we called out a greeting, all three of us. Selena walked to the spot where the sounds had come from. She saw nobody, but sensed a very definite presence . . . .

The darkness was now silent. I felt exposed and helpless.

Then the footsteps resumed, this time walking off into the underbrush and apparently over a cliff! We waited, but there was no crash below. Two other people had seen odd manifestations earlier that evening, one a lighted disk sailing along beneath cloud cover, the other a ball of fire bouncing through a meadow.[22]

Reading such an account, can there be any doubt in the reader's mind that Strieber's occultic involvements are directly connected to his abduction experiences? I don't believe for a minute that Strieber came into contact with bona fide aliens from outer space. Rather, he came into contact with demonic spirits who were posing as aliens. What happened to Strieber is precisely what has happened to many others who have involved themselves in the occult.

I find it interesting that Strieber himself has noticed in his own investigations that people who have had abduction experiences tend to *develop* occultic powers (we noted this phenomenon in the previous chapter). He writes that "precognition, apparent telepathy, out-of-the-body perceptions, and even physical levitation are commonplace side-effects of contact with the visitors. I find this absolutely astonishing, but I cannot deny it."[23] Indeed, Strieber says, "thousands of letters and personal interviews with people who have encountered them—with many of them reporting one or more of these effects—convince me that they are a real outcome of contact."[24]

Let the reader beware. Involvement in occultism may lead to an experience similar to—*if not worse than*—that experienced by Whitley Strieber. And any contact with alleged "aliens" (who are really demons) will likely draw one deeper into the occult. It is a vicious and deadly downward spiral! No wonder God so harshly condemned occultism in Scripture (Deuteronomy 18).

— 11 —

Demonized Delusions
in the End Times

Gordon Creighton, editor of the British journal *Flying Saucer Review*, admits that "there seems to be no evidence yet that any of these craft or beings originate from outer space."[1] Not only is there no scientific evidence that UFOs come from outer space, but there are scientific problems that make such a view highly unlikely.

Bernard Oliver, the chief of research for Hewlett-Packard, spoke at a symposium conducted by NASA. Researcher Mark Albrecht summarized Oliver's main point this way:

> He pointed out that the nearest star, Alpha Centauri, which is four light years away, represents an 80,000-year round trip from earth with our present technology. Beyond that, it is unlikely that any star within 100 light years distance is stable enough to support bio-chemical evolution.[2]

This would seem to militate against extraterrestrials visiting planet Earth from outer space. The distance is just too vast to make this a feasible possibility.

Furthermore, as Christian apologists John Ankerberg and John Weldon point out:

> In light of the messages given by the UFO entities, how credible is it to think that literally thousands of genuine extraterrestrials would fly millions or billions of light years simply to teach New Age philosophy, deny Christianity, and support the occult? *Why would they do this with the preponderance of such activity already occurring on this planet?* And why would the entities actually possess and inhabit people just like demons do if they were really advanced extraterrestrials? Why would they consistently lie about things we know are true and purposely deceive their contacts?[3]

I noted earlier that many UFO sightings have a natural explanation. Other sightings may involve deliberate hoaxes. Hence, I don't want to imply that every time someone sees an unidentified flying object Satan is at work. However, as I suggested in the chapters on occultism, I think a case can be made that those UFOs that remain *truly unidentifiable*—and especially those that make "contact," or communicate messages to human beings, or "abduct" people—are rooted in the work of Satan. Let me explain why I think this is a viable possibility.

Anti-Christian/Pro-New Age Message

The messages communicated by the alleged extraterrestrials consistently go against biblical Christianity. As Christian researcher Ralph Rath puts it, "There is nothing in the UFO phenomena that leads to the belief in the one true God. There is much in the UFO phenomena, on the other hand, that contradicts the ideas of God as revealed in the Bible and Christian tradition."[4]

David Wimbish agrees with Rath, and affirms: "We cannot believe Jesus *and* the visitors because their claims contradict one another. There is no way to reconcile the two."[5] Indeed, Wimbish notes:

> The visitors are perfectly in tune with what has become known as "New Age" religion—Eastern mysticism, astral projection, the harmonic convergence, and so on. They are not at all in harmony, though, with Jesus Christ, who said, "I am the way, the truth, and the life." At the very least, they are more interested in steering us away from the truth of the Bible than toward it.[6]

We have already discussed in great detail the extremely strong link between the UFO phenomenon and occultism. We have also noted that the messages received from "extraterrestrials" typically come through occultic means, such as channeling or automatic handwriting.

UFO contactees and abductees are often involved in a number of other forms of occultism, including the Ouija board, tarot cards, psychometry (psychic messages derived from touching personal articles), palm reading, seances, aura reading, crystal ball gazing, astrology, and much more. After encountering UFOs, people are often drawn even further into the world of the occult, such as out-of-body experiences and various forms of psychic phenomena.[7]

Where there is the occult, there is demonism. Where there is demonism, there is the occult. One naturally goes with the other, just as surely as darkness accompanies night.

Demons Against God

Experts who have long investigated UFOs—both Christian and non-Christian—have noted the strong similarity of the

UFO experiences and typical manifestations of demonism.[8] Brooks Alexander, of the Spiritual Counterfeits Project, commented on the *John Ankerberg Show:*

> A lot of the characteristics that attend UFO "close encounters" are also highly characteristic of demonic encounters . . . . More than anything else, the thing that we came to understand was that these UFOs are not extraterrestrial space vehicles, but they are extradimensional beings.[9]

John Keel, a respected authority on UFOs, said that "the UFO manifestations seem to be, by and large, merely minor variations of the age-old demonological phenomenon." Moreover, "the manifestations and occurrences described in [the literature of demonology] are similar, if not entirely identical, to the UFO phenomenon itself. Victims of [demon] possession suffer the very same medical and emotional symptoms as the UFO contactees."[10]

In his book *Communion*, Whitley Strieber (whom we discussed in the previous chapter) made comments indicating his own perception of the presence of the demonic:

> Increasingly I felt as if I were entering a struggle for my soul, my essence, or whatever part of me might have reference to the eternal . . . . There are worse things than death, I suspected. And I was beginning to get the distinct impression that one of them had taken an interest in me. So far the word *demon* had never been spoken among the scientists and doctors who were working with me. And why should it have been? We were beyond such things. We were a group of atheists and agnostics, far too sophisticated to be concerned with such archaic ideas as demons and angels.[11]

Strieber continues:

> I felt an absolutely indescribable sense of menace.
> It was hell on Earth to be there, and yet I couldn't
> move, couldn't cry out and couldn't get away. I lay
> as still as death, suffering inner agonies. Whatever
> was there seemed so monstrously ugly, so filthy
> and dark and sinister. Of course they were
> demons. They had to be. And they were here and
> I couldn't get away. I couldn't save my poor family.
> I still remember that thing crouching there, so ter-
> ribly ugly, its arms and legs like the limbs of a great
> insect, its eyes glaring at me.[12]

In keeping with this, Jacques Vallee, in his book *Messengers of Deception*, observes an "impressive parallel" between
"UFO occupants and the popular conception of demons."[13]
Vallee says that "the UFO beings of today belong to the same
class of manifestation as the [demonic] entities that were described in centuries past."[14]

In a U.S. Government official document entitled *UFOs
and Related Subjects: An Annotated Bibliography*, Lynn E. Catoe
said:

> A large part of the available UFO literature is closely
> linked with mysticism and the metaphysical. It deals
> with subjects like mental telepathy, automatic writ-
> ing, and invisible entities, as well as phenomena like
> poltergeist ["noisy spirit"] manifestations and pos-
> session . . . Many of the UFO reports now being
> published in the popular press recount alleged inci-
> dents that are strikingly similar to demonic posses-
> sion and psychic phenomena which has long been
> known to theologians and parapsychologists.[15]

Former New Ager Randall Baer likewise affirms:

> From millions of New Agers' experiences, there is a profoundly potent force behind whatever the UFOs really are. That force is definitely demonic in nature and has extraordinary delusionary brainwashing effects on people. I believe that, whatever new information may be uncovered about this phenomena in the years ahead, UFOs are messengers of deception, nothing else.[16]

It is also highly revealing that these so-called "extraterrestrials" engage in modes of contact with human beings that are essentially the same as those of other types of entities in the world of the occult: departed spirits, fallen angels, fairies, Ascended Masters, and various interdimensional beings. Dr. Hugh Ross, Christian astronomer, confirms from his research that people who have had contact with UFOs suffer the same kinds of physical, mental, emotional, and spiritual symptoms as those who have been demon-possessed. And the greater the degree of occult involvement in one's background, the higher the chance of a UFO encounter of some kind.[17]

Joe Jordan, a state director for the Mutual UFO Network (MUFON), agrees, noting that "the similarity between the abduction experience and demonic possession is very, very close." He believes that "these [alien contact] experiences these people are having are real. It does exist. But you just need to understand what's doing it."[18] That is, people need to understand that *demons* are doing it. "This whole thing is spiritual warfare. And the method the enemy's using is deception. Strong deception."[19]

In support of the idea that UFOs may in fact be manifestations of Satan or demons is the belief by some individuals that the UFOs themselves are *alive*. Brad Steiger, who has written a number of books on the UFO phenomenon, said: "I have even come to suspect that in some instances, what we have been calling 'spaceships' may actually be a form of higher intelligence rather than vehicles transporting occupants."[20] Likewise, John Keel noted that "over and over again, witnesses have told me in hushed tones, 'You know, I don't think that thing I saw was mechanical at all. I got the distinct impression that it was alive.'"[21]

If it is true that these manifestations are actually living beings and not material spaceships—and if in fact these "living beings" are powerful demonic spirits, which I believe them to be—then this may help us to understand how these entities can seemingly take off at incredible speeds, go thousands of miles per hour, and turn at 45-degree angles without even slowing down. We know that angels have the capability of flying, some of them very swiftly (Daniel 9:21). If angels have this ability, we must assume that demons have this capability as well, since demons are nothing more than fallen angels.

Moreover, the apostle Paul in 2 Thessalonians 2:9 tells us that Satan has the ability to work "all kinds of counterfeit miracles, signs and wonders." This verse certainly indicates that Satan has the ability to pull off the UFO deception.

Interestingly, Jacques Vallee, cited previously, also notes that a fifteenth-century French calendar, known as the *kalendrier des Bergiers,* portrayed demons piercing their victims' abdomens with long needles.[22] "Let us recall that, while under hypnosis, Betty Hill [a UFO abductee] reported that a long needle was inserted into her navel, causing great pain," Vallee observed.[23] "To find alien abduction parallels in primitive magic, mythology, occultism, and the fairy-faith, all one has to do is remove one's blinders and look."[24] For this reason, one researcher has concluded that UFOs are actually ISAs—*Identifiable as Satanic Apparitions.*[25]

Can Demons Take On a Physical Appearance?

In an earlier chapter I noted the possibility that for those already involved in the occult, Satan may blind their minds and in some way induce a mystical dreamlike experience in their minds in which they "perceive" that they are being abducted (though they are not actually *physically* abducted)—a dream that is later "recalled" or "remembered" by means of hypnosis as being a "true event." I feel there is a lot of merit to this explanation. But it is also possible that in abduction episodes, demons are actually taking on a physical appearance in the guise of "aliens."

Some readers may resist the idea that demons can actually take on some kind of an appearance, since they are spirit beings. However, the biblical evidence indicates that spirit beings *can* take on an appearance. Angels, for example, are spirit beings (Hebrews 1:14), but can nevertheless appear as men (Matthew 1:20; Luke 1:26; John 20:12). Their resemblance to men can be so realistic, in fact, that they are actually taken to be human beings (Hebrews 13:2).

Recall from the Old Testament that Abraham welcomed three "men" in the plains of Mamre (Genesis 18:1-8). These "men" walked, talked, sat down, and ate—just like normal men—but they were not men; they were angels (see Genesis 18:22; 19:1). Now we have no scriptural evidence that angels need food for sustenance. But apparently they can appear as men and eat like men during the course of fulfilling their assigned task in the realm of humanity.

We also know from Scripture that demons are simply fallen angels. Revelation 12:7 even makes reference to "the dragon and his angels." In context, the dragon is Satan. Satan heads up a vast group of fallen angels, also known as demons (Matthew 12:24).

If good angels have the capacity to take on a physical appearance, what is to stop fallen angels from doing the same?

They are fallen, yes, but they still have the same angelic constitution (nature) as the good angels. Hence, if good angels have that capacity, we must conclude that evil angels have that capacity as well.

Don't get me wrong; I'm not saying demons take on an appearance all the time. I believe that demons, like the holy angels, work behind the scenes most of the time in the spirit world. My point is that there is nothing scripturally to forbid demonic fallen angels from taking on a physical appearance during abduction episodes. As a professor at Wheaton College put it, "Demons are fallen angels according to Scripture . . . . Angels can appear to people. It would seem you could argue demons could, too."[26]

Merrill Unger, in his book *Demons in the World Today*, speaks of the connection between spiritism and the materialization of demonic spirit entities. "Perhaps the most remarkable phenomena of spiritism are materializations. These are supernatural appearances and disappearances of material images in connection with the activities of a spiritistic medium." Unger argues that such materializations are to be considered lying signs and wonders performed by Satan (2 Thessalonians 2:8-10; Revelation 13:15).[27]

Since people who typically go through abduction experiences have a history of occultic involvement, it could very well be that during abduction episodes a demonic entity "materializes" much in the same way that materializations occur in spiritistic contexts. Such a scenario cannot be easily dismissed in view of the evidence.

Abductions Halted in Jesus' Name

UFO researchers Joe Jordan (of MUFON) and Wes Clark say they have verifiable cases in which apparent abduction experiences were *halted* in the name of Jesus. Jordan says there may be as many as 400 such cases documentable nationwide.[28]

"It makes you wonder—If these beings are extraterrestrial at all, why would they respond to that name?" Jordan asks. "We think we found the answer in the Bible, in Mark 16:17, where Jesus said, 'In my name they shall cast out demons.' That seems to be exactly what we came across."[29]

According to Jordan, three other UFO researchers informed him (off the record) that they had come across similar cases. "They were afraid for their credibility," Jordan says. "They felt they already had put their credentials out far enough dealing with extraterrestrials."[30]

One abductee reported: "I thought I was having a satanic experience, that the Devil had gotten hold of me and had shoved a pole up my rectum and was holding me up in the air . . . so helpless. I couldn't do anything."[31] This abductee was actually a nonreligious person, but he had been to church a few times with his wife. He recollects that when he encountered this experience—

> I said, "Jesus, Jesus, help me," or, "Jesus, Jesus, Jesus!" And when I did, there was a feeling or a sound or something. That either my words that I had thought, or the words that I had tried to say or whatever, hurt whatever was holding me up in the air on this pole.[32]

The abductee reports that as he appealed to the name of Jesus, "I felt like [the object] was withdrawn, and I fell. I hit the bed, because it was like I was thrown back in the bed. I really can't tell what it was. But when I did, my wife woke up and asked why I was jumping on the bed."[33]

If indeed these entities respond to the name of Jesus, does this not give us a strong clue about the true identity of these "extraterrestrials"? The fact that these entities cease their evil deeds when the authority of Jesus—the Lord of the universe—

is appealed to adds an exclamation point to the evidence already presented that they are in reality demonic spirits.

These Entities are "Interdimensional"

Another key evidence that these "aliens" are not from outer space but are rather demonic spirits is the view of many researchers that instead of coming from outer space, these entities seem to appear from another dimension. J. Allen Hynek, author of *The UFO Experience: A Scientific Inquiry*, notes that "if one wishes to postulate worlds other than the physical (astral or etheric), one can easily satisfy and explain virtually all the reported antics of the UFO."[34]

Perhaps Jacques Vallee, more than any other researcher, has written about this aspect of the alien intruders. Vallee's research, which has been going on for decades now, had led him to believe (as a non-Christian) that these aliens and UFOs are real but that they are more likely from other dimensions than from other planets.[35] "The UFO occupants, like the elves of old, are not extraterrestrials. They are denizens of another reality."[36] Indeed:

> I believe that the UFO phenomenon represents evidence for other dimensions beyond space-time; the UFOs may not come from ordinary space, but from a multiverse which is all around us, and of which we have stubbornly refused to consider the disturbing reality in spite of the evidence available to us for centuries.[37]

What are some of the contributing factors to this conclusion? To begin with, Vallee cites the ability of these objects to seemingly materialize on the spot—very abruptly, out of nowhere, as it were—as a key evidence.[38] These objects sometimes seem to have a ghostly, apparitionlike demeanor—sometimes giving indication of having the ability to "float" through solid matter.[39] Further, even though these entities seem to appear out of another dimension, Vallee says "this does not exclude a material physical presence at the time of the sighting."[40]

Of course, we must acknowledge that many of the non-Christian investigators of the UFO phenomenon are not thinking of demonic spirits when they write about interdimensional beings. In their view, there may be some kind of parallel universe with living populations much like our own.

Richard Hall, in his book *Uninvited Guests: A Documented History of UFO Sightings, Alien Encounters, & Cover-ups*, explains the theory this way:

> Somewhat more appealing, though an equally fuzzy concept in many respects, is the idea of parallel universes. Essentially this suggests multiple existences of sentient lifeforms who somehow share the same or overlapping Space-Time with us. They differ from us primarily in consisting of matter of a different density, or perhaps variable density. Sometimes, according to this view, the natural environment is right for them to become visible to us and vice versa. Or, through technology, they are able to manipulate the environment in order to interact with us . . . .
>
> It is fun to imagine a parallel universe populated by the UFO beings who one day discovered us. Perhaps their society had a history of ghost and apparition reports (pooh-poohed by their scientists), or our atomic tests sent detectable particles into their realm. Anyway, at some point in their evolution they developed the science and technology that allowed them to manipulate matter, and

lo and behold they discovered the existence of a parallel universe . . . .

The essence of the concept is that sentient lifeforms consisting of masses of different densities exist in parallel and, either naturally or by technological manipulation, sometimes are changed to a roughly corresponding level so that they become visible and tangible to each other.[41]

Some New Age occultists have a similar view to this, but add an "etheric" twist to it. Benjamin Creme, for example, wrote in his book *The Reappearance of the Christ and the Masters of Wisdom*:

An essential fact to bear in mind in relation to UFOs is that they are etheric in nature . . . . What we see is the result of their ability to lower the vibrational rate of themselves, or their vehicles, temporarily, to a level where we can see them and know them.[42]

These may be terms the reader is unfamiliar with. As I point out in my book *The Counterfeit Christ of the New Age Movement*, occultists believe an etheric earth exists behind the physical earth. The etheric earth is thought to be made up of a fine energy substance from which is created the mold for every form that is manifested in the physical plane. Every material object on the physical plane has an etheric counterpart. All material forms in the physical universe find their ultimate source in this energy substance of the etheric realm.[43]

In Creme's thinking, the UFOs find their actual home in the etheric plane. Etheric entities (such as aliens and UFOs) are essential spirits in nature, and are viewed as having a "high" vibrational rate—vibrating so fast that you can't normally see them. It's kind of like looking at the blades of a fan when the fan is on. You can essentially see through the fan because the blades are spinning so fast. In the same way, occultists believe that etheric entities have such a high vibrational rate that you can't see them—that is, unless they slow down their vibrational rate so they take on physical appearance. As Timothy Green Beckley, author of *Psychic and UFO Revelations in the Last Days,* puts it, "in order to land, the [alien] visitors have to transmute or lower their frequency vibration into our third dimensional level, to appear solid."[44]

All of this discussion is simply to say that there are both respected researchers (such as Jacques Vallee) and New Age occultists (such as Benjamin Creme) who are saying that their research indicates that these "aliens" and "UFOs" are actually coming to us from another dimension. And when they appear, they seem to materialize out of nowhere. When they materialize, they seem to actually take on physical characteristics.

Here is the important connection I want you to see: We know that God's good angels (who are spirit beings) live in the spirit dimension around us, and that they have the capability of taking on a physical appearance, as they did when they appeared to Abraham in Genesis 18. Demons, who are fallen angels, also live in the spirit dimension (a "parallel universe" of sorts) and apparently have the capability of taking on a physical appearance.

It is my belief that even though Vallee and Creme (and others who have suggested the interdimensional theory) are not Christians, their research ultimately gives support for the view of many Christians that these alien entities are actually demonic spirits who are appearing from the spirit realm to various human beings—and the human beings they typically "appear" to are those who have been involved in some form of the occult. These could be *actual* appearances (materializations), or they could be what one might call *psychic* appearances in contexts where a person involved in the occult is in a mystical "altered state of consciousness" and "perceives" or "sees" an entity, though that entity is not physically there.

Demonized Delusions in the End Times

The diabolical goal of these "aliens" appears to be severalfold. They seek not only to keep those presently involved in the occult enslaved to occultism, but they also seek to draw people deeper into the occult. Further, the revelations that these beings are giving people foster a New Age (anti-Christian) worldview—a worldview that says "All is one," and we are evolving toward perfection, and the space brothers are here to help us as we enter into a New Age.

These entities have also come up with a counterfeit endtimes theology, which says there is coming a day when the "rapture" will occur, with UFOs swooping down to take "the faithful" (UFO enthusiasts) off the planet. This will be followed by a period of cleansing, and then a New Age of enlightenment and harmony will begin.

Ultimately, I believe that the diabolical goal of these entities is to set forth a massive end-time delusion as we draw near the second coming of Christ—a delusion that will keep as many people as possible from turning to the true Savior, Jesus Christ. As Paul McGuire put it:

> It appears that Satan has devised a strategy to blind this generation from the good news of Jesus Christ by capturing their minds with a New Age philosophy that incorporates a belief in UFOs and aliens. People are being taught to watch the heavens, not for a coming Messiah who will judge the world and establish His kingdom, but for celestial beings who breed a powerful spiritual deception. [45]

My friend William Alnor, who has done some excellent research on UFOs, has commented that religious leaders are alarmed about a growing train of thought that "wants us to reject traditional Judeo-Christian ideas about God" in favor of benign "space brothers" who will save humanity from itself.[46] Alnor believes—and I agree with him—that this new belief is a setup for apocalyptic deceptions predicted in the Bible's book of Revelation.[47]

Over the past few decades, it would appear that our planet has been undergoing a conditioning process in which people are being made more and more open to the possibility of alien contact. News reports, TV specials, and TV series focusing on UFOs have become extremely popular. Hundreds of such books have been written, many of them making the *New York Times* bestseller list. There are multiple magazines and newsletters dealing with the UFO phenomenon. Major motion pictures about alien encounters produced by some of Hollywood's top film moguls have become blockbusters. As never before, people the world over have been conditioned to accept UFOs *as real*. And the more people who accept UFOs as real, the easier it will be to explain away true biblical rapture when it occurs.

Signs from Heaven?

A verse that is sometimes quoted by Christian researchers of the UFO phenomena is Luke 21:11, where Jesus, speaking of the end times, said: "There will be great earthquakes, famines and pestilences in various places, and fearful events *and great signs from heaven*." Could it be that the "signs from heaven" includes the appearances of UFOs? Some think so. The Greek word "*semeion*," it is pointed out, literally means, "an unusual occurrence, transcending the common course of nature."[48] In this context, it is argued that the word "heavens" refers not to God's domain but rather to the skies above us. So, it is argued, perhaps the verse at least includes the possibility of UFO phenomena.

There are also those who believe the book of Revelation may give us some clues about UFOs. It is pointed out that in Revelation 12, some time prior to the second coming of Christ, the archangel Michael and the holy angels will do battle with Satan and his fallen angels, and Satan will lose the battle. He and the fallen angels will be ousted from heaven and "hurled to the earth" (see verse 9). Even though this is a spiritual battle, it is suggested by some that perhaps there are some physical manifestations to it (such as UFO appearances).[49]

Some on the more sensational side have gone so far as to suggest the possibility of an actual (Satan-created) landing of a UFO in the end times. While I personally find such a suggestion almost impossible to swallow, some think it would be the ultimate delusion for an unbelieving world. Second Thessalonians 2:11 is often cited in support of this view: "For this reason God sends them a powerful delusion so that they will believe the lie." Hal Lindsey is an advocate of this scenario:

> There is going to come a time in our age when God is going to permit all those on Earth who are unsaved to be deceived by some great wonder. This deception will close their minds and hearts to the truth of God's Word.
>
> We're already seeing many people deceived today by all manner of false doctrines. But I believe this passage refers to something even more dramatic. I think it might be pointing to something along the lines of the scenarios in *Childhood's End* or *The Day the Earth Stood Still.*
>
> I could be wrong, but I think it is very possible for demons to stage a spacecraft landing on Earth, probably claiming they are from an advanced

civilization from another part of the universe. This is about the only thing colossal enough to cause Hindus, Moslems, Buddhists, false Christians, et al., to forget old differences and get together into a one world religion . . . .

Judging from some of the wild counterfeit creation theories being spread today, they may even claim to have been the race that "planted" human life on this planet. They may tell us they are here to check up on our progress and steer us on a better course—prepare us for some great "quantum leap" forward.[50]

Whether or not one agrees with such a speculative theory, one can agree that demonic spirits acting in the guise of aliens are presently involved and will continue to be involved in end-time delusions. See my books *The New Age Movement* (Zondervan Publishing House) and *The Counterfeit Christ of the New Age Movement* (Baker Book House), for other New Age end-time scenarios.

What About Genesis 6?

Another area of great speculation and controversy relates to the record of events in Genesis 6:4: "There were giants in the earth in those days; and also after that, when the sons of God came in unto the daughters of men, and they bore children to them, the same became mighty men which were of old, men of renown" (KJV). Some in the New Age movement believe this verse means that aliens came down and cohabited with human women, giving rise to a hybrid race of giants.

Although Christian thinkers unanimously reject the "alien" theory, the meaning of Genesis 6:4 is a matter of wide debate among evangelicals. One popular theory is expounded by Christian writer Paul McGuire (among others), who tells us that some Bible scholars believe that in the days of Noah, just before the coming of the flood, fallen angels visited the earth and engaged in sexual relations with women, producing a unique hybrid offspring that the Bible refers to as "the Nephilim" (giants).[51] These Bible scholars believe that this interbreeding of fallen angels and human women was a contributing factor to God's sending of the flood. Jude 6,7 makes reference to some angels "which kept not their first estate, but left their own habitation" (KJV). It is argued that this leaving "their first estate" refers to crossing the angelic boundary by engaging in relations with human women.

Other Christian scholars believe that some fallen angels *possessed* real human beings (that is, demon possession), who then cohabited with the daughters of men. This view has the merit of providing a good explanation of how angels, who are bodiless (Hebrews 1:14) and sexless (Matthew 22:30), could cohabit with human women.

Still another common interpretation to this passage is that the sons of God are simply the godly line of Seth (the Redeemer's line—Genesis 4:26), who intermingled with the godless line of Cain. Bible scholar Gleason Archer notes:

> Instead of remaining true to God and loyal to their spiritual heritage, they allowed themselves to be enticed by the beauty of ungodly women who were daughters of men—that is, of the tradition and example of Cain. In support of this view is the fact that human beings are sometimes called sons (Isaiah 43:6).[52]

The point I am making, then, is that we should not build too much of a theological belief (or a belief about UFOs) on the foundation of a verse that is so widely disputed among evangelicals. Besides, there are plenty of other *clear* passages of

Scripture that give us keen insights into the UFO phenomena. I have cited many of these throughout this book.

Regardless of the Genesis 6 issue, this chapter has demonstrated that there is more than enough evidence to conclude that the "aliens" presently appearing to human beings are nothing more than evil demonic spirits intent on deceiving humanity. For this reason, it is more important than ever for Christians to be discerning about the UFO phenomenon. *Don't be fooled by deceiving spirits!*

12

The Rise of Doomsday Shivers

A string of zeros on time's odometer suggests that global changes are coming, and they're going to be dramatic and sudden.

—Ted Daniels, founder of
Millennium Watch Institute[1]

In the last thirty years [the UFOs] have been accelerating their interaction with us in preparation for a fast-approaching time of transition and transformation.

—Brad Steiger, New Ager[2]

One need not strain to whiff the scent of burgeoning apocalyptic enthusiasms. Flying-saucer cultists, paramilitary survivalists, prophets of ecodeath (death of the environment), Nostradamean sages, and others are spouting out millennial doomsday prophecies faster than anyone can count them.[3]

An astute observer of the times has remarked that "clearly, we have now entered the 'hot zone' of millennial time . . . in which hopes and expectations are raised to a fever pitch and believers sustain a maximum level of missionary and preparatory activity."[4]

So strong are the millennial jitters in this country that TV anchorman Peter Jennings said on *World News Tonight*:

> The coming millennium is generating a lot of excitement around the globe, not all of it good. For some groups, the year 2000 is the trip-wire for the end of the world—call it apocalyptic anxiety, if you will. It isn't new, of course. But in the age of technology, doomsday has taken on a whole new twist.[5]

In agreement with Jennings, one writer noted that "as the year 2000 looms, end-of-the-world-as-we-know-it fears seem to be intensifying—fears of global pollution, holes in the ozone layer, nuclear war, natural disasters, plagues like AIDS that don't respond to Western medicine."[6] This country does indeed seem to have the millennial jitters.

Richard Landes, a professor of Medieval History at Boston University and Director of the independent Center for Millennial Studies, comments:

> The religious cases go from obvious to surprising—Christians of all stripes who really believe that 2000 will mark either the Rapture or the Parousia (second coming of Christ); Muslims who believe that Christians and Jews plan to build the Third Temple in 2000 . . . even some Jews who think that Christianity was only given 2000 years of dominion over their people; and now a sect of Hindus who anticipate the beginning of the Kalki avatar, the final avatar of Vishnu who will become the world ruler in 1999–2003.

Beyond the denominational, we have readers

of Nostradamus's prophecies, Aquarian New Agers, Hopi Prophets and UFOlogists, even CEOs, government officials, and all those racing against the clock to render our computers "millennium compliant" before 2000.[7]

How is all this relevant to a study of UFOs? The answer is quite simple. As we will soon see, in examining the situation in the world at the turn of the first millennium, many people expected that the end was near. The same is true today. As we continue to draw near the year A.D. 2000, more and more people—including millions of UFO enthusiasts—believe this year signals either the end of man or the beginning of a Utopia, depending on whom you talk to.

I have included this chapter specifically to heighten Christians' awareness about millennial matters so they will maintain an attitude of discernment and sober-mindedness during these critical years. While this chapter deals with more than just UFOs, the UFO issue is most definitely a critical component in many people's millenarian scenarios. And it is the premise of this chapter that the best way to prepare for the future turn of the millennium is to understand what happened at the turn of the previous millennium.

Millennial Madness, Act 1 (A.D. 1000)

It seems that people have been predicting either imminent doom or glorious apocalypse since the pharaohs ruled Egypt. One example of this is what allegedly occurred at the turn of the first millennium. Legend and lore has it that near the close of the first millennium humanity became grievously afflicted with millennial fever. Consider the following account:

Toward the arrival of the last millennium—December 31, 999 A.D.—so many people in the Christian lands of that time actually thought that the world was coming to an end that they proceeded to act in an unaccustomed fashion. In their dealings with each other they became so brotherly, so charitable, so filled with self-abnegation and love for their neighbor that the true millennium, however briefly, seemed to be at hand.[8]

Men forgave their neighbors debts; people confessed their infidelities and wrongdoings. Farm animals were freed as their owners prepared for the final judgment.... The churches were besieged by crowds demanding confession and absolution. Commerce was interrupted. Beggars were liberally fed by the more fortunate. Prisoners were freed, yet many remained—wishing to expiate their sins before the end. Pilgrims flocked to Jerusalem from Europe. Class differences were forgotten. Slaves were freed....

Christmas passed with a splendid outpouring of love and piety. Food shops gave away food and merchants refused payment. Of course, when December 31st approached a general frenzy reached new heights. In Rome, Pope Sylvester II held midnight mass in the Basilica of St. Peters to a standing room only audience. But they weren't standing. All lay on their knees praying.

After the mass had been said, a deathly silence fell. The clock kept on ticking away its last minutes as Pope Sylvester raised his hands to the sky. The attendees at this time lay with their faces to the ground listening to the tick tick tick.

Suddenly the clock stopped. Several bodies, stricken by fear, dropped dead as the congregation began screaming in terror. Just as it had suddenly stopped ticking the clock resumed to meet the midnight hour. Deathly silence still reigned until the clock ticked past 12. Bells in the tower began to scream jubilantly. Pope Sylvester stretched out his hands and gave a blessing over his flock. When the *Te Deum* had been sung, men and women fell in each other's arms, laughing and crying and exchanging the kiss of peace.

Not long after the suspense at St. Peter's and elsewhere, life resumed its normal rhythm. Owners captured their once freed animals. Merchants ceased giving away their goods. Prisoners were captured to be placed back in the slammer. Debts were remembered. And life went on as if nothing happened.[9]

Did all of this really occur around A.D. 1000? One might think so from all the articles and books that have appeared in recent years popularizing the idea.[10] However, when one digs deep for hard, indisputable historical evidence, one is less than satisfied.[11] The question that arises is this: If a widespread panic and hysteria had really occurred, wouldn't we have more than the surviving 12 or 13 accounts of what happened at the turn of the first millennium—only half of which mention apocalyptic panics?[12]

Raoul Glaber, a Burgundian monk born in the late tenth century, wrote *Histories*—considered by many to be a prime source for what went on at the turn of the millennium. His writings indicate a panic concerning the approaching end.[13] A number of historians, however, have disputed Glaber's work.[14]

Moreover, historians interpret Glaber and other available writings of the time (few though they be) in different ways. For example, some "antipanic" analysts cite the fact that "people of the time wrote wills and testaments, clearly indicating an awareness of a future. But, note others, opening clauses of many of the surviving wills begin with some version of 'The end of the world being close, I hereby . . .' or 'The world coming to its conclusion, I . . .'"[15] Who is to say what all this meant, since lines such as these were merely standard, boilerplate openers for legal documents of that day?[16]

Despite all the confusion, I think we can say with a fair degree of certainty that while there probably was no mass hysteria or panic at the close of the first millennium, there *was* widespread concern that the end of the world might be near. A number of highly respected scholars support this view, noting that people living at the close of the first millennium had a definite case of the "preapocalyptic shivers."

For example, Reformed scholar Louis Berkhof, in his *History of Christian Doctrines*, confirms that—

> In the tenth century there was a widespread expectation of the approaching end of the world . . . . It was associated with the idea of the speedy coming of Antichrist. Christian art often chose its themes from eschatology. The hymn *Dies Irae* sounded the terrors of the coming judgment, painters depicted the end of the world on the canvas, and Dante gave a vivid description of hell in his *Divina Commedia*.[17]

Philip Schaff, in his highly respected *History of the Christian Church*, gives a flavor of the times when he said that Pope Sylvester II (who lived around A.D. 1000) gave "the first impulse, though prematurely, to the crusades at a time when hundreds of pilgrims flocked to the Holy Land in expectation of the end of the world after the lapse of the first Christian millennium."[18]

Stanley J. Grenz, in his well-received book, *The Millennial Maze*, said:

Repeatedly church history has witnessed times of increased speculation concerning the end and the advent of a golden age on earth. The approach of the year A.D. 1000, for example, caused a great stir of expectations. When both that year and A.D. 1033 (a thousand years after Christ's death) passed, interest turned to A.D. 1065, for in that year Good Friday coincided with the Day of the Annunciation. Multitudes journeyed to Jerusalem to await the Lord's return, some arriving already during the previous year and waiting in the Holy City until after Easter.[19]

Grenz also notes that Augustine's various statements concerning the meaning of the millennium mentioned in Revelation 20 were not void of ambiguity. Indeed, Grenz says that—

they could be (and were) readily understood to indicate that Christ's Second Coming should occur one thousand years after his first advent. This implicit prediction, carrying as it did the authority of the bishop of Hippa coupled both with the theme of the old age of the world and with a rise in political and natural disasters, resulted in a great sense of anticipation in parts of Christendom first as A.D. 1000 and then as A.D. 1033 approached.[20]

In his in-depth study, Henri Focillon concluded: "We have established that in the middle of the tenth century there existed a movement, a groundswell of the belief that the world was drawing to a close."[21] And "once the terminal year of the millennium has passed, the belief in the end of the world spreads with renewed vigor in the course of the eleventh century."[22] Though recognizing this "groundswell," Focillon is careful to point out that there was no mass hysteria, as some of the legendary accounts of the time seem to indicate.

To sum up, then, at the turn of the first millennium there was no mass hysteria but there definitely was widespread concern by many people that the end of the world was approaching. Here is my point in raising all of this: Just as many people were concerned about the end of the world around the turn of the first millennium, even so many are now concerned about the approach of the year A.D. 2000. Some believe that the end of the world may be near, while others believe that a glorious Utopia awaits us. And many believe that UFOs play a central role in how all this will unfold in the coming years. Let us now turn our full attention to the approach of A.D. 2000.

Millennial Madness, Act 2 (A.D. 2000)

Some today are predicting imminent doom, others a glorious Utopia, and still others predict doom followed by Utopia, under the leadership of "space brothers" aboard UFOs. Any way you look at it, millennial madness is on the rise. Though I'm not a prophet, I predict that this particular form of madness will afflict a significant share of the human race over the next few years.

I am not alone in this viewpoint. Cultural commentator Christopher Lasch says:

> As the twentieth century approaches its end, the conviction grows that many other things are ending too. Storm warnings, portents, hints of catastrophe haunt our times. The "sense of ending," which has given shape to so much of twentieth century literature, now pervades the popular imagination as well.[23]

Bible scholar Stanley Grenz likewise says:

> At the close of the twentieth century the message of the doomsday preachers—once the brunt of jokes and the laughingstock of "enlightened" citizens of the modern world—has become in the minds of many people a serious possibility and a genuine concern in a way unparalleled in prior decades. For the first time in recent history we sense that our civilization is tottering on the edge of a precipice peering into the abyss of self-destruction and chaos.[24]

Ken Carey, author of several New Age handbooks, envisions A.D. 2000 as a kind of psychic watershed. Beyond this time lies "a realizable utopian society" in which people will have "a real sense of a new beginning."[25] Professor Bruce Epperly of Georgetown University commented that "people are looking for a New Age, a new order of the world. They're looking for transformation. They're looking for the death of one world and the birth of another."[26]

David Spangler, another New Ager, agrees, and he points to a Central American prophecy connected with the Mayan and Aztec civilizations that predicts a time of great cleansing in our time. Following this, a New Age of harmony and wholeness will emerge. Spangler says, "The Hopi Indians of the American Southwest have a similar prophecy, also focused on the period from 1980 to 2000 A.D. as a time of transition into a new cycle of cooperation."[27] In several of his books, Spangler has acknowledged the role of the "space brothers" as all of this unfolds.

Elizabeth Clare Prophet, controversial New Age leader of the Church Universal and Triumphant (CUT), says she has been informed by an "Ascended Master" that catastrophe awaits the world. She has been saying for years that Russia will invade the United States: "I believe that anytime between now and 2002 there is a high probability, a likelihood, of a war between the United States and the Soviet Union."[28] In view of this, Prophet and her followers have built large bomb shelters to house the faithful. Church members can purchase room in the shelters for $6000 to $10,000 apiece.[29] Mrs. Prophet likens the shelters to Noah's ark in the earth.[30]

The idea that UFO phenomena will increase as we draw near the year 2000 is not the opinion of a mere handful of observers. It is rather the thoughtful consensus of almost everyone who has seriously looked at the issue.

Hugh Downs, of the ABC news program *20/20,* has concluded that "UFO-mania is alive and well. And, as the millennium approaches it will probably grow."[31]

Aaron M. Katz, of the Center for Millennial Studies, says that "a quick search of the World Wide Web will reveal hundreds of sites related to alien speculation, many of which contain highly detailed analyses (proofs) of impending planetary doom. These themes are also prevalent in many New Age books and magazines."[32]

John E. Pike, director of space policy at the Federation of American Scientists, agrees, noting that doomsday scenarios involving aliens reflect "a combination of all the zeroes on the odometer starting to line up, coupled with the various social and cultural dislocations that normally provide a fertile ground for millennial and apocalyptic expectations."[33]

Jacques Vallee, cited often in this book, made the following remarks about UFOs and the new millennium:

> As we reach the Millennium, the belief in the imminent arrival of extraterrestrials in our midst is a fantasy that is as powerful as any drug, as revolutionary as any delusion that marked the last

millennium, as poisonous as any of the great irrational upheavals of history.[34]

Ruth Montgomery, well-known for her books, believes
that the aliens aboard UFOs have the mission of awakening
humanity to the realization that their final destruction is imminent unless world leaders can come up with better ways of
settling disputes between nations. She believes the Earth is
going to shift on its axis in the year 2000, with catastrophic results, including the death of most of the people on Earth. The
aliens aboard UFOs, however, will save many of the more enlightened of Earth's population by evacuating them in galactic
fleets and later returning them to Earth for its rehabilitation
and recolonization.[35]

More recently, following the release of the hit movie
Contact, interviews were conducted among people living in
Orange County, California, near where I live. Many of the
people pointed out the significance of the approaching millennium, and its relationship to aliens and UFOs. "People are
searching for meaning in their lives, especially as we near the
millennium," one moviegoer said. "*Contact* speaks to that."

Some observers have noted that as we continue to draw
near to the year 2000, Hollywood continually seeks to produce
new and more exciting programs that "explore the mysteries
of creation and the meaning of life."

"I think there's more of an interest in science fiction as
we approach the millennium," says D.C. Fontana, one of television's top science fiction writers, whose long list of credits
includes *The Six Million Dollar Man, Logan's Run,* and *Star Trek.*
Fontana believes "there's a rise in superstition and feelings [as
we] change into a new century."

The approaching millennium seems to have filmmakers
probing the cosmic unknown at a furious pace. Recent years
have witnessed the production of such films as *Independence*

Day, Mars Attacks, Fifth Element, and *Men in Black,* several of which touch on the questions that have baffled humankind for centuries: Where did we come from? Why are we here? Are we alone?

The Search for Meaning

As we approach the new millennium, it seems that more than just Hollywood is seeking answers to the questions, Where did we come from? Why are we here? Are we alone? People the world over are searching for meaning.

How sad that as we draw near the end of this millennium, so many people are turning to the skies for answers instead of to the One who created the skies and all else in the universe. How tragic that so many are turning to what they perceive to be "space brothers" when in fact they have fallen victim to demonic spirits who seek to destroy them. As we draw near the close of the millennium, you and I as Christians must be ready to share the fact that only our Creator-God can give us the answers to life's deepest questions.

Where did we come from? Man is not the result of alien seed. Our race wasn't planted here by extraterrestrials. God created the Earth and then created man to dwell upon the earth (Genesis 1). God created man from the dust of the ground and then breathed the breath of life into him (Genesis 2:4-7). And how awesome a moment it must have been. At one moment no man existed; the next moment, there he stood.

Why are we here? We have not been placed here and then guided by extraterrestrials as we evolve toward building our own Utopia on Earth. We are here *by God's* design. We are here to glorify God and fellowship with Him forever. God created us with a capacity to know and fellowship with Him. Our purpose—indeed, our highest aim in life—should be to know God. "This is what the LORD says: 'Let not the wise man boast of his wisdom or the strong man boast of his strength or the rich man boast of his riches, but let him who boasts boast about this: that he understands and knows me'" (Jeremiah 9:23,24).

Are we alone? Never. God will always be with us, as will His holy angels. When God created Adam, He declared Adam's loneliness to be "not good" (Genesis 2:18). God made man as a social being. Man was not created to be alone. He was created to enter into and enjoy relationships with other people and with God.

We must not forget that there is a hunger in the heart of man that *none but God* can satisfy, a vacuum that *only God* can fill. We were created with a need for fellowship with God. And we are restless and insecure until this becomes our living experience. A counterfeit spirituality—one based on revelations from "space brothers"—will not do. Only God can fill this void. Until a person comes into the relationship with God that he was created for, the void will remain ever-present. This is the most important message we can bring people as the millennial fever escalates.

13

Against the Darkness

I'll never forget the first time I experienced an earthquake in Southern California. The ground started moving beneath my feet. Everything was in motion. I heard creaking sounds all around me as my sturdy house swayed back and forth. The lamp hanging from the ceiling by a chain swayed to and fro. The water in the cat's bowl splashed over the sides.

Then it was over. It lasted only about seven seconds, but seven seconds is an awfully long time when everything around you is moving.

My wife, Kerri, and I immediately turned on the television, only to discover that the earthquake we had just experienced was actually rather mild. It only registered about a 4 on the Richter scale. But if that was mild, I thought to myself, I'd sure hate to go through a big earthquake.

Later that evening we learned from television news reports that no one had been hurt in the earthquake, and there was no substantial damage to houses or businesses in the area. But, as usual, the newscasters used this opportunity to remind viewers that though this earthquake was mild, the "Big One" was coming in the next 30 years or so, and people had better be prepared for it.

You see, in a powerful earthquake, the ground not only

moves violently, but it can last for minutes at a time. In such an earthquake the damage can be catastrophic. Foundations of houses and buildings can be severely damaged or destroyed. Sturdy structures can crumble to the ground like a house of cards.

For the last few decades, America has been experiencing a powerful earthquake—that is, a *worldview* earthquake. What is a "worldview"? It is a way of viewing or interpreting the world around us. It is an interpretive framework through which we can make sense out of the data of life and the world.[1] In the last 30 years, the way Americans look at and interpret the world has changed dramatically. The worldview "sands" have been shifting beneath our very feet.

One of the ways our worldview has shifted is that we have swung toward a new openness to the paranormal and the occult. In fact, the occult has become mainstream in America, and things are going to get worse in coming years. Psychic phenomena is here to stay, it appears, and for this reason it is more important than ever for Christians to have their spiritual defenses in place.

Because earthquakes are common in Southern California, most houses are structurally designed and built to withstand the shaking and swaying that is characteristic of earthquakes. Let us learn a lesson here. As Christians, we must make sure our *spiritual* foundation is built so that assaults on our worldview—such as those coming from the world of the occult, currently manifested in the phenomenally popular UFO movement—will not crumble our spiritual lives (see Matthew 7:24-27). Christians will either be strong in the power of the Lord's might or they will become casualties (Ephesians 6:10-13).

Christ's Warning of Deception
The winds of change are continuing to blow on the religious

landscape in America today, and its effects should signal concern in the heart of every Christian. As the ominous dark clouds continue to gather on the horizon, with stories of UFOs and alien encounters continuing to surface, many Christians go merrily on their way, oblivious to what is going on around them. Better to heed the warning of Jesus!

Jesus clearly cautioned His followers about religious deception in the last days: "At that time many will turn away from the faith and will betray and hate each other, and many false prophets will appear and deceive many people" (Matthew 24:10,11). Earlier, Jesus had warned His followers to "watch out for false prophets. They come to you in sheep's clothing, but inwardly they are ferocious wolves" (Matthew 7:15). As I have shown in this book, the so-called extraterrestrials seek to appear as benevolent "brothers," but in fact they are ferocious demonic wolves who seek to lead us astray.

The apostle Paul sternly warned, "Satan himself masquerades as an angel of light. It is not surprising, then, if his servants masquerade as servants of righteousness" (2 Corinthians 11:14). The fact is that *appearances can be deceiving.* This is why we need to anchor ourselves in the absolutes of the Word of God.

The apostle John instructs us:

> Do not believe every spirit, but test the spirits to see whether they are from God, because many false prophets have gone out into the world. This is how you can recognize the Spirit of God: Every spirit that acknowledges that Jesus Christ has come in the flesh is from God, but every spirit that does not acknowledge Jesus is not from God. This is the spirit of the antichrist, which you have heard is coming and even now is already in the world (1 John 4:1-3).

By these verses alone, the extraterrestrials fail in terms of being messengers from the true God. Consider what we have learned in this book:

- A key goal of the "aliens" is to change the way human beings think about God and His Word (the Bible), and to replace exclusivistic Christianity with a religion of universalism.
- The "aliens" never say anything that *affirms* the Bible as being God's Word.
- The "aliens" never say anything that even remotely glorifies Christ.
- The "aliens" never say anything about man's sin problem and a need for redemption.
- The "aliens" never say anything about Christ's redemptive work at the cross.
- The "aliens" offer blasphemous reinterpretations of the incarnation of Christ—suggesting, for example, that aliens injected Mary with the sperm of a space creature from another world. Others suggest that Jesus Himself came from another planet.
- "Revelations" from these so-called "space brothers" not only consistently contradict the Scriptures but consistently promote a New Age worldview.
- "Revelations" from these entities set forth a satanic counterfeit end-times scenario involving a "rapture" (which is a false counterpart to the genuine rapture), a time of cleansing (a false counterpart to the great tribulation), and a New Age of enlightenment and harmony (a false counterpart to Christ's future millennial kingdom).
- This counterfeit end-times scenario is in perfect keeping with how Satan counterfeits the truth in so many other ways: Satan has his own *church*—the "synagogue of Satan" (Revelation 2:9); he has his own *ministers*—ministers of darkness who bring false sermons (2 Corinthians 11:4,5); he has formulated his own

system of theology—called "things taught by demons" (1 Timothy 4:1); his ministers proclaim his *gospel*—"a gospel other than the one we preached to you" (Galatians 1:7,8); he has his own *throne* (Revelation 13:2) and his own *worshipers* (Revelation 13:4); he inspires *false Christs* and self-constituted *messiahs* (Matthew 24:4,5); he employs *false teachers* who bring in "destructive heresies" (2 Peter 2:1); he sends out *false prophets* (Matthew 24:11); and he sponsors *false apostles* who imitate the true (2 Corinthians 11:13).

• It is typically people who are already involved in the occult who have abduction experiences.

• People who have abduction experiences typically get drawn *even further* into the occult, including the development of psychic powers, clairvoyance, psychokenesis, automatic handwriting, channeling, levitation, and out-of-body experiences.

• The abduction experiences reported by many people today are similar in many ways to the experiences of those who have undergone occultic shamanistic initiation ceremonies.

• Researchers have consistently noted that these alleged aliens seem to come out of nowhere, from another dimension. This would be in perfect keeping with a demonic manifestation.

• These UFOs sometimes have ghostly, apparitionlike qualities, seemingly able to float through solid objects. This would be consistent with the spiritual nature of demons.

• Some researchers have concluded that the UFOs are not mechanical spacecrafts at all, but are rather living beings (which would be consistent with demonic manifestations).

• These "aliens" cease abduction attempts at the name of Jesus. This too is consistent with what we know from Scripture (see Matthew 17:18; Mark 9:25).

By "testing the spirits" (1 John 4:1-3), as the apostle John instructs us to do, it becomes quite clear that these "alien entities" are in fact demonic spirits intent on deceiving humankind (2 Corinthians 11:14; see also 2 Thessalonians 2:9-12). Scripture unmasks these entities for who they really are—malevolent lying spirits.

Flexing Apologetic Muscle in an Age of UFOs

When we talk about Christian apologetics, we are not talking about Christians apologizing for their faith, or feeling sorry for their beliefs. "Apologetics" comes from the Greek word *apologia,* which means "defense."

In view of what I have shared in this book about UFOs, it is obvious that the need for apologetics today is critical. Believers must realize that we are living in a post-Christian era, with a host of religions, cults, and occultic systems vying continuously for people's commitments and indeed for their very lives. The newest occultic challenge is from outer space—and the challenge is real! We must face the challenge head-on.

Apologetics provides well-reasoned evidences why people ought to choose Christianity rather than any other religion—such as those offered by UFO enthusiasts (Urantia, Heaven's Gate, the Aetherius Society, and the Raelian Society, for example). Apologetics demonstrates that all the other options in the smorgasbord of religions are not really options at all, since they are false.

Apologetics provides not only a defense for the faith, but it also provides security to Christians who need to be sure that their faith is not a blind leap into a dark chasm, but is rather *faith founded on fact.* Apologetics demonstrates *why* we believe *what* we believe. Apologetics does not *replace* our faith but *grounds* our faith. Frankly, with so many Christians undiscerningly buying into the UFO craze *hook, line, and sinker,* apologetic answers on the UFO phenomena are much needed today. That is why I wrote this book.

Prepared to Give Answers

Scripture exhorts Christians to always be prepared to give people reasons why they believe the way they do. First Peter 3:15 says: "*Always* be prepared to give an answer to everyone who asks you to give the reason for the hope that you have. But do this with gentleness and respect."

The only way to be *always prepared* to give an answer to everyone is to become equipped with apologetic answers. In regard to the UFO phenomena, the book you are holding in your hands has hopefully equipped you with what you need to know to be able to provide needed answers to people who are starving for truth in our society. Your answers can make a difference. *So be bold and speak the truth in the face of the occultic intruder.*

It is truly unfortunate that many Christians today seem to be "secret-agent" Christians who have never "blown their cover" before an unregenerate world. The fact is that many Christians have little or no impact on their world for Christ or for Christian values.

Many such Christians have a hideous disease, which Dr. Walter Martin appropriately labeled *non-rock-a-boatus*. This disease has so effectively neutralized Christians that the cancer of occultism has been free to spread at an incredible, unprecedented pace in America. The UFO movement, remember, is the current craze in movies, TV, books, magazines, and more. Christians everywhere should speak the truth about what is really going on.

Unfortunately, Christians today seem to be so fearful of "rocking the boat" that they clam up and keep their Christianity to themselves. They think that if they speak forth for Christ and for Christian values in this predominantly anti-Christian (and occult-oriented) culture, they may offend someone or perhaps be ridiculed and embarrassed.

If this disease continues unchecked, you can count on the continued deterioration of America as well as the continued growth of the occult. If Christians do not act, those involved in the occult *will* act. The war is on, and you as a Christian will be either a soldier in the midst of the conflict or a casualty on the sidelines. *Which will it be?*

—— Appendices ——

Throughout this book I have argued that the "aliens," "extraterrestrials," and "space brothers" are actually manifestations of Satan and his host of demons. But who are Satan and his demons? And how can we as Christians stand against them? What should unbelievers do?

Appendix A: Who Is Satan?

Appendix B: Who Are Demons?

Appendix C: The Christian's Defense
                   Against Fallen Angels

Appendix D: If You're Not a Christian . . .

—— Appendix A ——

Who Is Satan?

Lucifer's Fall

Satan's name at one time was Lucifer. Lucifer was originally created as a magnificent angel of God. But he sinned and rebelled against God. Lucifer's fall is described in two key Old Testament chapters—Ezekiel 28 and Isaiah 14. Let's briefly look at both of these.

It would seem from the context of Ezekiel 28 that the first ten verses of this chapter are dealing with a human leader. Then, starting in verse 11 and on through verse 19, Lucifer is the focus of discussion.

What is the rationale for the conclusion that these latter verses refer to the fall of Lucifer? Whereas the first ten verses in this chapter speak about the *ruler* of Tyre (who was condemned for claiming to be a god though he was just a man), the discussion moves to the *king* of Tyre, starting in verse 11. Many scholars believe that though there was a human *ruler* of Tyre, the real *king* of Tyre was Satan, for it was he who was ultimately at work in this anti-God city and it was he who worked through the human ruler of the city.

Some have suggested that these verses may actually be dealing with a human king of Tyre that was *empowered* by

Satan. Perhaps the historic king of Tyre was a tool of Satan, possibly even indwelt by him. In describing this king, Ezekiel also gives us glimpses of the powerful creature Satan, who was using, if not indwelling, the king of Tyre.

Now there are things that are true of this "king" that—at least ultimately—are simply not true of human beings. For example, the king is portrayed as having a *different nature* from man (he is a cherub—verse 14); he had a *different position* from man (he was blameless and sinless—verse 15); he was in a *different realm* from man (the holy mount of God—verses 13,14); he received a *different judgment* from man (he was cast out of the mountain of God and thrown to the earth—verse 16); and the superlatives used to describe him don't seem to fit that of a normal human being (full of wisdom, perfect in beauty, and having the seal of perfection—verse 12).

Our text tells us that this king was a created being and left the creative hand of God in a perfect state (Ezekiel 28:12,15). And he remained perfect in his ways until iniquity was found in him (verse 15b). What was this iniquity? We read in verse 17, "Your heart became proud on account of your beauty, and you corrupted your wisdom because of your splendor." Lucifer apparently became so impressed with his own beauty, intelligence, power, and position that he began to desire for himself the honor and glory that belong to God alone. The sin that corrupted Lucifer was self-generated pride.

Apparently this represents the actual beginning of sin in the universe—preceding the fall of the human Adam by an indeterminate time. Sin originated in the free will of Lucifer in which—with full understanding of the issues involved—he chose to rebel against his Creator.

This mighty angelic being was rightfully judged by God: "I threw you to the earth" (Ezekiel 28:17). This doesn't mean that Satan had no further access to heaven, for other Scripture verses clearly indicate that Satan maintained a certain amount of access even after his fall (Job 1:6-12; Zechariah 3:1,2). However, Ezekiel 28:18 indicates that Satan was absolutely and completely cast out of God's heavenly government and place of authority (compare Luke 10:18).

Isaiah 14:12-17 is another Old Testament passage that may refer to the fall of Lucifer. We must be frank in admitting that some Bible scholars see no reference whatsoever to Lucifer in this passage. It is argued that the personage mentioned in this verse is referred to as a man (Isaiah 14:16) and is compared with other kings on the earth (verse 18), and that the words "How you have fallen from heaven" (verse 12) simply refer to a fall from great political heights.

There are other scholars who interpret this passage as referring *only* to the fall of Lucifer, with no reference whatsoever to a human king. The argument here is that the description of this being is beyond humanness, and hence could not refer to a mere mortal man.

There is a third view that I think is preferable to the two views above. This view sees Isaiah 14:12-17 as having a dual reference. It may be that verses 4 through 11 deal with an actual king of Babylon. Then, in verses 12 through 17, we find a *dual* reference that includes not just the king of Babylon but a description of Lucifer as well.

If this passage contains a reference to the fall of Lucifer, then the pattern of this passage would seem to fit that of the Ezekiel 28 reference—that is, first a human leader is described, and then dual reference is made to a human leader *and* Satan.

It is significant that the language used to describe this being fits other passages in the Bible that speak about Satan. For example, the five "I wills" in Isaiah 14 indicate an element of pride, which was also evidenced in Ezekiel 28:17 (compare 1 Timothy 3:6, which makes reference to Satan's *conceit*).

As a result of this heinous sin against God, Lucifer was

banished from living in heaven (Isaiah 14:12). He became corrupt, and his name was changed from *Lucifer* ("morning star") to *Satan* ("adversary"). His power became completely perverted (Isaiah 14:12,16,17). And his destiny, following the second coming of Christ, is to be bound in a pit during the thousand-year millennial kingdom over which Christ will rule (Revelation 20:3), and eventually to be thrown into the lake of fire (Matthew 25:41).

How Scripture Describes Satan

The Bible speaks about Satan in a variety of ways. We learn much about Satan and his work by the various names and titles used of him. For example:

- Satan is called our *adversary* (1 Peter 5:8 KJV). This word indicates that Satan opposes us and stands against us in every way he can.
- Satan is called the *devil* (Matthew 4:1). This word carries the idea of "adversary" as well as "slanderer." The devil was and is the adversary of Christ; he is the adversary of all who follow Christ. Satan slanders God to man (Genesis 3:1-5), and man to God (Job 1:9; 2:4). (A slanderer is a person who utters maliciously false reports that injure the reputation of another.[1])
- Satan is called our *enemy* (Matthew 13:39). This word comes from a root meaning "hatred." It characterizes Satan's attitude in an absolute sense. He hates both God and His children.
- Satan is called the *evil one* (1 John 5:19). He is "the opposer of all that is good and the promoter of all that is evil."[2] Indeed, he is the very embodiment of evil.
- Satan is called the *father of lies* (John 8:44). The word "father" is used here metaphorically of the originator of a family or company of persons animated by a deceitful character. Satan was the first and greatest liar.

• Satan is called a *murderer* (John 8:44). This word literally means "man killer" (compare 1 John 3:12,15). Hatred is usually the motive that leads one to commit murder. Satan hates both God and His children, so he has a genuine motive for murder. Ray Stedman notes that "because he is a liar and a murderer, the Devil's work is to deceive and to destroy. There you have the explanation for all that has been going on in human history throughout the whole course of the record of man . . . . Whom the Devil cannot deceive, he tries to destroy, and whom he cannot destroy, he attempts to deceive."[3]

• Satan is called the *god of this age* (2 Corinthians 4:4). Of course, this does not mean that Satan is deity. It simply means that this is an evil age, and Satan is its "god" in the sense that he is the head of it. As well as "god of this age," Satan is in "back of the false cults and systems that have cursed the true church through the ages."[4]

• Satan is called the *prince of the power of the air* (Ephesians 2:2 KJV). It would seem that the "air" in this context is the sphere in which the inhabitants of this world live. This sphere represents the very seat of Satan's authority.

• Satan is called the *prince of this world* (John 12:31; 14:30; 16:11). The key word here is "world." This word refers not to the physical earth but to "a vast order or system that Satan has promoted which conforms to his ideals, aims, and methods."[5]

• Satan is called a *roaring lion* (1 Peter 5:8,9). This graphic simile depicts Satan's strength and destructiveness.

• Satan is called the *tempter* (Matthew 4:3). "This name indicates his constant purpose and endeavor to incite man to sin. He presents the most plausible excuses and suggests the most striking advantages for sinning."[6]

• Satan is called a *serpent* (Genesis 3:1; Revelation 12:9). This word symbolizes the origin of sin in the Garden of Eden, as well as the hatefulness and deadly effect of sin. The serpent is characterized by treachery, deceitfulness, venom, and murderous desires.

• Satan is called *Beelzebub* (Matthew 12:24). This word literally means "lord of the flies," carrying the idea "lord of filth." The devil corrupts everything he touches.

• Satan is called the *accuser of our brethren* (Revelation 12:10 KJV). The Greek tense of this verse indicates that accusing God's people is a continuous, ongoing work of Satan. He never lets up. This verse indicates that Satan accuses God's people "day and night." Thomas Ice and Robert Dean note that "Satan opposes God's people in two ways. First, he brings charges against believers before God (Zechariah 3:1; Romans 8:33). Second, he accuses believers to their own conscience."[7]

From this brief survey of names, it becomes clear that Satan's avowed purpose is to thwart the plan of God in every area and by every means possible. Toward this end, Satan promotes a world system of which he is the head and which stands in opposition to God and His rule in this universe. His latest strategy involves UFOs and "space brothers."

Appendix B

Who Are Demons?

Who are the demons? If Satan's fall is described in Ezekiel 28 and Isaiah 14, as Appendix A indicates, are there any references in the Bible to the fall of numerous angels who became demons? I believe there are some hints in Scripture that help us answer this question.

Many scholars believe the first five verses of Revelation 12 contain a minihistory of Satan. In keeping with this, it would seem that Revelation 12:4 refers to the fall of the angels who followed Satan: "His [Satan's] tail swept a third of the stars out of the sky and flung them to the earth."[1] It has long been recognized that the word "stars" is sometimes used of angels in the Bible (compare Job 38:7). If "stars" refers to angels in Revelation 12:4, it would appear that after Lucifer rebelled against God, he was able to draw a third of the angelic realm after him in this rebellion. When he sinned, he did not sin alone, but apparently led a massive angelic revolt against God.

Just a few verses later we read of the "dragon *and his angels*" (Revelation 12:7; compare Ephesians 3:10; 6:12). There is little doubt that demons are simply fallen angels.[2] Elsewhere in the Bible Satan (himself a fallen angel) is called "the prince of the demons" (Matthew 12:24). Demons are Satan's emissaries to promote his purpose to thwart the plan of God.

The demons are highly committed to their dark prince, Satan. Indeed, "these spirits, having [made] an irrevocable choice to follow Satan instead of remaining loyal to their Creator, have become irretrievably confirmed in wickedness and irreparably abandoned to delusion. Hence, they are in full sympathy with their prince, and render him willing service in their varied ranks and positions of service in his highly organized kingdom of evil."[3]

Demons are portrayed in Scripture as being thoroughly wicked. They are designated "unclean spirits" (Matthew 10:1 KJV), "evil spirits" (Luke 7:21), and "spiritual forces of evil" (Ephesians 6:12). All these terms point to the immoral nature of demons. It is not surprising, then, that many people involved in the occult are involved in immorality.[4]

What kinds of wicked things do demons do? Among many other things, Scripture portrays them as inflicting physical diseases on people (such as *dumbness*—Matthew 9:33; *blindness*—12:22; and *epilepsy*—17:15-18). They also afflict people with mental disorders (Mark 5:4,5; 9:22; Luke 8:27-29; 9:37-42). They cause people to be self-destructive (Mark 5:5; Luke 9:42). They are even responsible for the deaths of some people (Revelation 9:14-19).

Of course, we must be careful to note that even though demons can cause physical illnesses, Scripture distinguishes natural illnesses from demon-caused illnesses (Matthew 4:24; Mark 1:32; Luke 7:21; 9:1; Acts 5:16). Theologian Millard J. Erickson notes that "in the case of numerous healings no mention is made of demons. In Matthew, for example, no mention is made of demon exorcism in the case of the healing of the centurion's servant (8:5-13), the woman with the hemorrhage of twelve years' duration (9:19,20), the two blind men (9:27-30), the man with the withered hand (12:9-14), and those who touched the fringe of Jesus' garment (14:35,36)."[5] Hence, every time you get sick you must not presume you are being afflicted by a demon.

Presently there are two classes or groups of demons. One group of demons is free and active in opposing God and His people (Ephesians 2:1-3). The other group of demons is confined. Charles Ryrie notes that—

> of those who are confined, some are temporarily so, while others are permanently confined in Tartarus (2 Peter 2:4 and Jude 6). The Greeks thought of Tartarus as a place of punishment lower than Hades. Those temporarily confined are in the abyss (Luke 8:31; Revelation 9:1-3,11), some apparently consigned there to await final judgment, while others will be loosed to be active on the earth [during the future seven-year Tribulation period] (verses 1-3,11,14; 16:14).[6]

Why are some fallen angels (demons) permanently confined? It seems reasonable to assume that they are being punished for some sin other than the original rebellion against God. Some theologians believe these angels are guilty of the unnatural sin mentioned in Genesis 6:2-4, and because of the gross depravity of this sin they are permanently confined to Tartarus.[7] Other theologians say we cannot know for sure what these demons did that caused their incarceration, but can only assume that they are especially vile.

Ranks Among Fallen Angels

The holy angels are organized according to rank (Colossians 1:16). The same is true among the fallen angels (Ephesians 6:12). Demons are organized according to rank—including *principalities, powers, rulers of the darkness of this world,* and *spiritual wickedness in high places.*[8] And all fallen angels, regardless of their individual ranks, follow the leadership of their malevolent commander-in-chief—Satan, the prince of demons.

The high degree of organization in the kingdom of darkness may sometimes make it seem like Satan is *omniscient* (all-knowing) and/or *omnipotent* (all-powerful). Demons report to Satan from all over the world, thereby extending his own reach and influence. But Satan is neither omniscient nor omnipotent. He is merely a creature with creaturely limitations.

Varying Degrees of Depravity

It would seem from the Scriptures that there are varying degrees of depravity among the fallen angels. Jesus spoke of a demon who left his abode but then returned, bringing with him "seven other spirits *more wicked than himself*" (Matthew 12:45 KJV, italics added). Clearly, then, Jesus Himself indicates that some demons are more evil than others. This would seem to be in line with the teaching that some demons have committed such depraved acts that they are presently imprisoned (2 Peter 2:4).

The Work of Fallen Angels Among Unbelievers

Second Corinthians 4:4 indicates that Satan blinds the minds of unbelievers to the truth of the gospel. This passage indicates that Satan inhibits the unbeliever's ability to think or reason properly in regard to spiritual matters.[9] It would seem that one of the ways Satan does this is by leading people to think that *any* way to heaven is as acceptable as another. In other words, Satan promotes the idea that one doesn't need to believe in Jesus Christ as the *only* means to salvation.

Satan also seeks to snatch the Word of God from the hearts of unbelievers when they hear it (Luke 8:12). Demons, under Satan's lead, seek to disseminate false doctrine (1 Timothy 4:1). As well, they wield influence over false prophets (1 John 4:1-4) and seek to turn people to the worship of idols (Leviticus 17:7; Deuteronomy 32:17; Psalm 106:36-38). Satan and demons also promote occultism and paranormal phenomena (see Leviticus

20:27; Deuteronomy 18:10,11; 2 Kings 21:6; Isaiah 8:19; 19:3; 29:4). In short, fallen angels do all they can to spread spiritual deception.

The Work of Fallen Angels Among Believers

Fallen angels are also very active in seeking to harm believers in various ways. For example:

- Satan tempts believers to sin (Ephesians 2:1-3; 1 Thessalonians 3:5).

- Satan tempts believers to lie (Acts 5:3).

- Satan tempts believers to commit sexually immoral acts (1 Corinthians 7:5).

- Satan accuses and slanders believers (Revelation 12:10).

- Satan hinders the work of believers in any way he can (1 Thessalonians 2:18).

- Satan and demons seek to wage war against and *defeat* believers (Ephesians 6:11,12).

- Satan sows "weeds" among believers (Matthew 13:38,39).

- Satan incites persecutions against believers (Revelation 2:10).

- Demons hinder answers to the prayers of believers (Daniel 10:12-20).

- Satan is said to oppose Christians with the ferociousness of a hungry lion (1 Peter 5:8).

- Satan seeks to plant doubt in the minds of believers (Genesis 3:1-5).

- Satan seeks to foster spiritual pride in the hearts of Christians (1 Timothy 3:6).

- Satan seeks to lead believers away from the simplicity and purity of devotion to Christ (2 Corinthians 11:3).

- Demons seek to instigate jealousy and factions among believers (James 3:13-16).

- Demons would separate the believer from Christ if they could (Romans 8:38).

- Demons cooperate with Satan in working against believers (Matthew 25:41; Ephesians 6:12; Revelation 12:7-12).

Quite obviously Satan and his demons are formidable opponents. As Appendix C makes clear, however, God has given us everything necessary for us to enjoy victory over the powers of darkness.

— Appendix C —

The Christian's Defense Against Fallen Angels

We as Christians should be very thankful that God has made provisions for our defense against Satan and his fallen angels. What does this defense consist of?

To begin with, we must always keep in mind that twice in the New Testament we are told that the Lord Jesus Christ lives in heaven to make intercession for us (Romans 8:34; Hebrews 7:25). In other words, Jesus prays for us on a regular basis. Certainly Christ's intercession for us includes the kind of intercession He made for His disciples in John 17:15, where He specifically asked the Father to keep them safe from the evil one.

Beyond this, God has provided spiritual armor for our defense (Ephesians 6:11-18). Each piece of armor is important and serves its own special purpose. But you and I must choose to *put on* this armor. God doesn't force us to dress in it. *We do it by choice.* Read Paul's description of this armor:

> Put on the *full armor* of God so that you can take your stand against the devil's schemes. For our struggle is not against flesh and blood, but against

217

the rulers, against the authorities, against the powers of this dark world and against the spiritual
forces of evil in the heavenly realms. Therefore put
on the *full armor* of God, so that when the day of
evil comes, you may be able to stand your ground,
and after you have done everything, to stand.

Stand firm then, with the *belt of truth* buck-
led around your waist, with the *breastplate of righteousness* in place, and with your *feet* fitted with
the readiness that comes from the gospel of peace.
In addition to all this, take up the *shield of faith,*
with which you can extinguish all the flaming ar-
rows of the evil one. Take the *helmet of salvation*
and the *sword of the Spirit,* which is the word of
God. And pray in the Spirit on all occasions with
all kinds of prayers and requests. With this in
mind, be alert and always keep on praying for all
the saints (italics added).

Without wearing this spiritual armor, you and I don't
stand a chance against the forces of darkness. But with this
armor on, victory is ours. "Wearing" this armor means that
our lives will be characterized by such things as righteousness,
obedience to the will of God, faith in God, and an effective use
of the Word of God. *These* are the things that spell DEFEAT for
Satan's attacks in your life. In effect, putting on the armor of
God amounts to putting on Jesus Christ, who Himself defeated
the devil. (Good books are available that fully explain how to
"put on" this spiritual armor.)[1]

Effective use of the Word of God is especially important
for spiritual victory. Jesus used the Word of God to defeat the
devil during His wilderness temptations (Matthew 4:1-11). We
must learn to do the same. Related to this, Pastor Ray Stedman
says, "Obviously, the greater exposure there is to Scripture the

more the Spirit can use this mighty sword in our lives. If you never read or study your Bible, you are terribly exposed to defeat and despair. You have no defense; you have nothing to put up against these forces that are at work. Therefore, learn to read your Bible regularly."[2]

Of course, Scripture specifically instructs us that each believer must be *informed* and thereby *alert* to the attacks of Satan (1 Peter 5:8). A prerequisite to defeating an enemy is to know as much as possible about the enemy—including his tactics. The apostle Paul says that we are not to be ignorant of his schemes (2 Corinthians 2:11). (One of his "schemes" today relates to UFO phenomena.) We find all the information we need about this enemy and his schemes in the Word of God.

We are also instructed to take a decisive stand against Satan. James 4:7 says, "Resist the devil, and he will flee from you." This is not a onetime resistance. Rather, on a day-to-day basis we must steadfastly resist the devil. And when we do, he will flee from us. Ephesians 6:13,14 tells us to "stand firm" against the devil. This we can do not in our own strength but in the strength of Christ. After all, it was Christ who "disarmed the powers and authorities . . . [and] made a public spectacle of them, triumphing over them by the cross" (Colossians 2:15).

We must not give place to the devil by letting sunset pass with us having unrighteous anger in our hearts toward someone (Ephesians 4:26,27). An excess of wrath in our heart gives opportunity to the devil to work in our lives.

We are instructed to rely on the indwelling Spirit of God, remembering that "the one who is in you is greater than the one who is in the world" (1 John 4:4).

We should pray for ourselves and for each other. Jesus set an example for us in the Lord's Prayer by teaching us to pray, "Deliver us from the evil one" (Matthew 6:13). This should be a daily prayer. Jesus also set an example of how to pray for others in His prayer for Peter: "Simon, Simon, Satan has asked to sift you as wheat. But I have prayed for you, Simon, *that your faith may not fail*" (Luke 22:31,32, italics added). We should pray for each other that we will maintain a strong faith in the face of adversity.

Of course, the believer should *never* dabble in the occult, for this gives the devil a great opportunity to work in our lives (Deuteronomy 18:10,11; compare Romans 16:19).

Finally, we must remember that Satan is "on a leash." He cannot go beyond what God will allow him (the book of Job makes this abundantly clear).[3] We should rest secure in the fact that God is in control of the universe, and that Satan cannot simply do as he pleases in our lives.

By following disciplines such as those outlined above, we will have victory over Satan and his host of demons who seek to bring us down. Remember, successfully defeating the powers of darkness does not rest upon what you can do in your own strength but upon what Christ has already done for you. You are more than a conqueror through Him that loved you (Romans 8:37).

———— Appendix D ————

If You're Not a Christian . . .

Perhaps you have read this book only because you have an interest in UFOs and aliens. It could be that you have even had some past involvement in some form of the occult. But maybe some of the Scriptures cited in this book have touched your heart. Now that you've read about the dangers of occultism and the counterfeit system of theology being promoted by Satan, perhaps God has moved it upon your heart to become a Christian. This appendix is for you. In it, I'll tell you how to become a Christian.

I want to begin by telling you that a personal relationship with Jesus is the most important decision you could ever make in your life. It is unlike any other relationship. For if you go into eternity without *this* relationship, you will spend eternity apart from Him.

So, if you will allow me, I'd like to tell you how you can come into a personal relationship with Jesus.

First you need to recognize that . . .

God *Desires* a Personal Relationship with You

God created you (Genesis 1:27). And He didn't just create you to exist all alone and apart from Him. He created you so that you would have a personal relationship with Him.

Remember, God had face-to-face encounters and fellowship with Adam and Eve, the first couple (Genesis 3:8-19). And just as God fellowshiped with them, so He desires to fellowship *with you* (1 John 1:5-7). God loves you (John 3:16). Never forget that fact.

The problem is . . .

Humanity Has a Sin Problem That Blocks a Relationship with God

When Adam and Eve chose to sin against God in the Garden of Eden, they catapulted the entire human race—to which they gave birth—into sin. Since the time of Adam and Eve, every human being has been born into the world with a propensity to sin.

The apostle Paul affirmed that "sin entered the world through one man, and death through sin" (Romans 5:12). Indeed, we are told that "through the disobedience of the one man the many were made sinners" (Romans 5:19). Ultimately this means that "death came through a man . . . in Adam all die" (1 Corinthians 15:21,22).

Jesus often spoke of sin in metaphors that illustrate the havoc sin can wreak in one's life. He described sin as *blindness* (Matthew 23:16-26), *sickness* (Matthew 9:12), being *enslaved in bondage* (John 8:34), and *living in darkness* (John 8:12; 12:35-46). Moreover, Jesus taught that this is a *universal condition* and that all people are guilty before God (Luke 7:37-48).

Jesus also taught that both inner thoughts and external acts render a person guilty (Matthew 5:28). He taught that from within the human heart come evil thoughts, sexual immorality, theft, murder, adultery, greed, malice, deceit, lewdness, envy, slander, arrogance, and folly (Mark 7:21-23). Moreover, He affirmed that God is fully aware of every person's sins, both external acts and inner thoughts; nothing escapes His notice (Matthew 22:18; Luke 6:8; John 4:17-19).

Of course, some people are more morally upright than

others. But we *all* fall short of God's infinite standards (Romans 3:23). In a contest to see who can throw a rock to the moon, I am sure a muscular athlete could throw the rock much farther than I could. But all human beings ultimately fall short of the task. Similarly, all of us fall short of measuring up to God's perfect holy standards.

Though the sin problem is a serious one, God has graciously provided a solution:

Jesus Died for Our Sins and Made Salvation Possible

God's absolute holiness demands that sin be punished. The good news of the gospel, however, is that Jesus has taken this punishment on Himself. God loves us so much that He sent Jesus to bear the penalty for our sins!

Jesus affirmed that it was for the very purpose of dying that He came into the world (John 12:27). Moreover, He perceived His death as being a sacrificial offering *for the sins of humanity* (Matthew 26:26-28). Jesus took His sacrificial mission with utmost seriousness, for He knew that without Him, humanity would certainly perish (Matthew 16:25; John 3:16) and spend eternity apart from God in a place of great suffering (Matthew 10:28; 11:23; 23:33; 25:41; Luke 16:22-28).

Jesus therefore described His mission this way: "The Son of Man did not come to be served, but to serve, and to give his life as a ransom for many" (Matthew 20:28). "The Son of Man came to seek and to save what was lost" (Luke 19:10); for "God did not send his Son into the world to condemn the world, but to save the world through him" (John 3:17).

But the benefits of Christ's death on the cross are not automatically applied to your life. God requires you to . . .

Believe in Jesus Christ

By His sacrificial death on the cross, Jesus took the sins of the entire world on Himself and made salvation available for everyone

(1 John 2:2). But this salvation is not automatic. Only those who personally choose to believe in Christ are saved. This is the consistent testimony of the biblical Jesus. Listen to His words:

- "For God so loved the world that he gave his one and only Son, that whoever *believes* in him shall not perish but have eternal life" (John 3:16).

- "For my Father's will is that everyone who looks to the Son and *believes* in him shall have eternal life, and I will raise him up at the last day" (John 6:40).

- "I am the resurrection and the life. He who *believes* in me will live, even though he dies" (John 11:25).

Choosing *not* to believe in Jesus, by contrast, leads to eternal condemnation: "Whoever *believes* in him is not condemned, but whoever *does not believe* stands condemned already because he has not believed in the name of God's one and only Son" (John 3:18).

Free at Last: Forgiven of All Sins

When you believe in Christ the Savior, a wonderful thing happens: God forgives you of all your sins. *All of them!* He puts them completely out of His sight. Ponder for a few minutes the following verses, which speak of the forgiveness of those who have believed in Christ.

- "In him we have redemption through his blood, the forgiveness of sins, in accordance with the riches of God's grace" (Ephesians 1:7).

- God said, "Their sins and lawless acts I will remember no more" (Hebrews 10:17).

- "Blessed is he whose transgressions are forgiven, whose sins are covered. Blessed is the man whose sin the LORD does not count against him and in whose spirit is no deceit" (Psalm 32:1,2).

- "For as high as the heavens are above the earth, so great is his love for those who fear him; as far as the east is from the west, so far has he removed our transgressions from us" (Psalm 103:11,12).

Such forgiveness is wonderful indeed, for none of us can possibly work our way into heaven, or be good enough to warrant God's good favor. Because of what Jesus has done for us, we freely receive the gift of salvation. It is a gift provided solely through the grace of God (Ephesians 2:8,9). And all of it is ours by simply believing in Jesus.

Don't Put It Off

It is a highly dangerous thing to put off turning to Christ for salvation, for you do not know the day of your death. What if it happens this evening? "Death is the destiny of every man; the living should take this to heart" (Ecclesiastes 7:2).

If God is speaking to your heart now, then *now* is your door of opportunity to believe. "Seek the LORD while he may be found; call on him while he is near" (Isaiah 55:6).

Follow Me in Prayer

Would you like to place your faith in Jesus for the forgiveness of sins, thereby guaranteeing your eternal place in heaven with Him? If so, pray the following prayer with me.

Keep in mind that it's not the prayer itself that saves you; it is the *faith in your heart* that saves you. So let the following prayer be a simple expression of the faith that is in your heart.

225

Dear Jesus:

I want to have a relationship with You. I know I can't save myself, because I know I'm a sinner.

Thank You for dying on the cross on my behalf. I believe You died *for me,* and I accept Your free gift of salvation.

Thank You, Jesus.

Amen.

Welcome to God's Forever Family

On the authority of the Word of God, I can now assure you that you are a part of God's forever family. If you prayed this prayer with a heart of faith, you will spend all eternity by the side of Jesus in heaven. Welcome to God's family!

If You've Been Involved in the Occult

If you've been involved in the occult, there are some additional things you should do.

• Repent of all previous involvement in the occult, for this is a sin against God (Deuteronomy 18:9-14). Verbally renounce the occult before God.

• From now on, avoid all forms of the occult, even forms you may (up to now) have considered harmless—such as reading astrology columns in the newspaper. Turn away from all forms of occultism forever.

• Destroy and/or throw away all occultic objects, books, or magazines—anything related to the occult.

• Break off relationships with other people involved in the occult. This is difficult, I know, but it is necessary. Those involved in the occult will try to sway you back in. Be kind to them, and share the gospel with them, but don't fellowship with them.

• Purchase a Bible and read from it daily. I suggest beginning with the Gospel of John, not only because it exalts Christ but because it shows Christ's victory over Satan. Read at least one chapter a day, followed by a time of prayer.

• Join a Bible-believing church immediately. Get involved in it. Share your background with the pastoral staff and follow their advice. Join a Bible study group at the church so you'll have regular fellowship with other Christians.

• *Very important:* At the church you join, arrange for a group of committed Christians to pray for you daily for a period of at least three months. You may be sensing some heavy spiritual warfare during this initial time, having just left the kingdom of darkness to become a Christian.

• I assume you've already read Appendix C: "The Christian's Defense Against Fallen Angels." Be sure to learn this well.

• Purchase and read *Overrun by Demons,* a book on spiritual warfare by Thomas Ice and Robert Dean (Harvest House Publishers). This book will help you immensely.

• Contact me so I can help you: Ron Rhodes, P.O. Box 80087, Rancho Santa Margarita, CA 92688.

Bibliography

Alnor, William. *UFOs in the New Age: Extraterrestrial Messages and the Truth of Scripture.* Grand Rapids: Baker Book House, 1992.

Baer, Randall N. *Inside the New Age Nightmare.* Lafayette, LA: Huntington House, 1989.

Berliner, Stanton T. Friedman, and Don Friedman. *Crash at Corona: The U.S. Military Retrieval and Cover-up of a UFO.* New York: Paragon House, 1992.

Blum, Howard. *Out There: The Government's Secret Quest for Extraterrestrials.* New York: Simon and Schuster, 1990.

Boa, Kenneth. *Cults, World Religions, and You.* Wheaton: Victor Books, 1979.

Brooke, Tal. *When the World Will Be As One.* Eugene, OR: Harvest House Publishers, 1989.

Bryan, C. *Close Encounters of the Fourth Kind: Alien Abduction, UFOs, and the Conference at MIT.* New York: Alfred A. Knopf, 1995.

Chandler, Russell. *Doomsday: The End of the World.* Ann Arbor, MI: Servant Publications, 1993.

_____. *Racing Toward 2001*. Grand Rapids: Zondervan Publishing House, 1992.

_____. *Understanding the New Age*. Dallas: Word Publishing, 1991.

Creme, Benjamin. *The Reappearance of the Christ and the Masters of Wisdom*. Los Angeles: The Tara Press, 1980.

Enroth, Ronald. *A Guide to Cults and New Religions*. Downers Grove, IL: InterVarsity Press, 1983.

_____. *The Lure of the Cults*. Downers Grove, IL: InterVarsity Press, 1987.

First Contact: The Search for Extraterrestrial Intelligence. Ed. Ben Bova. New York: Nal Books, 1990.

Geisler, Norman L. and Jeff Amano. *The Infiltration of the New Age*. Wheaton: Tyndale House Publishers, 1990.

Geisler, Norman, and William Watkins. *Worlds Apart: A Handbook on World Views*. Grand Rapids: Baker Book House, 1989.

The Gods Have Landed: New Religions from Other Worlds. Ed. James R. Lewis. New York: State University of New York Press, 1995.

Groothuis, Douglas. *Confronting the New Age*. Downers Grove, IL: InterVarsity Press, 1988.

Hall, Richard. *Uninvited Guests: A Documented History of UFO Sightings, Alien Encounters, and Coverups*. Santa Fe: Aurora Press, 1988.

Hunt, Dave. *The Cult Explosion*. Eugene, OR: Harvest House Publishers, 1978.

Hynek, J. Allen. *The UFO Experience: A Scientific Inquiry*. Chicago: Henry Regnery Company, 1972.

Keel, John. *UFOs: Operation Trojan Horse*. New York: G. P. Putnam's Sons, 1970.

Larson, Bob. *Larson's Book of Cults*. Wheaton: Tyndale House Publishers, 1983.

Lindsey, Hal. *Planet Earth—2000 A.D.* Palos Verdes, CA: Western Front, 1994.

Lutzer, Erwin W., and John F. DeVries. *Satan's "Evangelistic" Strategy for This New Age.* Wheaton: Victor Books, 1991.

Mack, John. *Abduction: Human Encounters with Aliens.* New York: Charles Scribner's Sons, 1994.

MacLaine, Shirley. *Dancing in the Light.* New York: Bantam Books, 1985.

_____. *It's All in the Playing.* New York: Bantam Books, 1987.

Mangalwadi, Vishal. *When the New Age Gets Old.* Downers Grove, IL: InterVarsity Press, 1992.

Martin, Walter. *Martin Speaks Out on the Cults.* Ventura, CA: Regal Books, 1983.

_____. *The Kingdom of the Cults.* Minneapolis: Bethany House Publishers, 1985.

_____. *The New Cults.* Ventura, CA: Regal Books, 1980.

_____. *The Rise of the Cults.* Ventura, CA: Regal Books, 1983.

Matrisciana, Caryl. *Gods of the New Age.* Eugene, OR: Harvest House Publishers, 1985.

McDonough, Thomas R. *The Search for Extraterrestrial Intelligence.* New York: John Wiley & Sons, Inc., 1987.

McDowell, Josh, and Don Stewart. *Understanding the Cults.* San Bernardino, CA: Here's Life Publishers, 1983.

Melton, J. Gordon, and George Eberhart. *The Flying Saucer Contactee Movement: 1950-1990.* Santa Barbara: Santa Barbara Centre for Humanistic Studies, 1990.

Montgomery, Ruth. *Aliens Among Us.* New York: Ballantine, 1986.

The New Age Rage. Ed. Karen Hoyt. Old Tappan, NJ: Revell, 1987.

Not Necessarily the New Age. Ed. Robert Basil. Buffalo: Prometheus Books, 1988.

Rhodes, Ron. *The Counterfeit Christ of the New Age Movement.* Grand Rapids: Baker Book House, 1990.

_____. *The Culting of America.* Eugene, OR: Harvest House Publishers, 1994.

_____. *The New Age Movement.* Grand Rapids: Zondervan Publishing House, 1996.

Ryerson, Kevin, and Stephanie Harolde. *Spirit Communication.* New York: Bantam, 1989.

Sagan, Carl. *Cosmos.* New York: Ballantine Books, 1985.

Sire, James. *Scripture Twisting: Twenty Ways the Cults Misread the Bible.* Downers Grove, IL: InterVarsity Press, 1980.

Spangler, David. *Links with Space.* Marina Del Rey, CA: DeVorss, 1976.

Steiger, Brad. *The Fellowship.* New York: Ballantine, 1989.

_____. *Gods of Aquarius: UFOs and the Transformation of Man.* New York: Berkley Books, 1983.

_____. *The UFO Abductors.* New York: Berkley, 1988.

Strieber, Whitley. *Communion: A True Story.* New York: Beech Tree Books, 1987.

_____. *Transformation: The Breakthrough.* New York: William Morrow, 1988.

Swenson, Orville. *The Perilous Path of Cultism.* Caronport, Saskatchewan, Canada: Briercrest Books, 1987.

Thomas, I.D.E. *The Omega Conspiracy: Satan's Last Assault on God's Kingdom.* Oklahoma City: Hearthstone Publishing, 1986.

Thompson, Keith. *Angels and Aliens: UFOs and the Mythic Imagination.* New York: Addison-Wesley Publishing Co., 1954.

Tucker, Ruth. *Another Gospel: Alternative Religions and the New Age Movement.* Grand Rapids: Zondervan Publishing House, 1989.

The UFO Phenomenon: Mysteries of the Unknown. Ed. Time-Life. Alexandria, VA: Time-Life Books, n.d.

Vallee, Jacques. *Confrontations: A Scientist's Search for Alien Contact*. New York: Ballantine, 1990.

_____. *The Invisible College*. New York: Dutton, 1975.

_____. *Messengers of Deception: UFO Contacts and Cults*. Berkeley: And Or Press, 1979.

_____. *Revelations: Alien Contact and Human Deception*. New York: Ballantine Books, 1991.

_____. *UFO Chronicles of the Soviet Union*. New York: Ballantine Books, 1992.

Weldon, John, and John Ankerberg. *Cult Watch: What You Need to Know About Spiritual Deception*. Eugene, OR: Harvest House Publishers, 1991.

Weldon, John with Zola Levitt. *UFOs: What on Earth Is Happening?* Irvine, CA: Harvest House Publishers, 1975.

White, Frank. *The SETI Factor*. New York: Walker and Company, 1990.

Wimbish, David. *Something's Going On Out There*. Old Tappan, NJ: Revell, 1990.

Notes

Introduction—Have We Been Visited?

1. William M. Alnor, *UFOs in the New Age: Extraterrestrial Messages and the Truth of Scripture* (Grand Rapids: Baker Book House, 1992), p. 84.
2. Bryan Woolley, "We've Got to Believe in Something," in *Dallas Morning News*, June 29, 1997, p. 1F.
3. Bob Waldrep, "Beam Me Up, Scotty," on Watchman Fellowship web site, 1995, downloaded from Internet.
4. Richard Kadrey, "UFOs," in *Compton's Online Encyclopedia*, 1997, downloaded from Internet.
5. James Oberg, "Space Encounters," in *The Omni Book of the Paranormal and the Mind*, ed. Owen Davies (New York: Kensington, 1983), pp. 107-13; cf. Alnor, *UFOs in New Age*, p. 79.
6. Paul McGuire, "Alien Invaders," in *Charisma* magazine web site, 1997, downloaded from Internet.
7. Alnor, *UFOs in New Age*, p. 35.
8. J. Allen Hynek, *The UFO Experience: A Scientific Inquiry* (Chicago: Henry Regnery, 1972), p. 10.
9. Bob Larson, *Larson's Book of Cults* (Wheaton: Tyndale House Publishers, 1983), p. 343.
10. Dennis Stacy, "A Short Introduction to UFOlogy," in *MUFON UFO Journal*, 1997, downloaded from Internet.
11. Hynek, *UFO Experience*, p. 29.
12. Ibid.
13. Ibid.
14. Waldrep, "Beam Me Up."

15. Paul McCarthy, "Close Encounters of the Fifth Kind: Communicating with UFOs," in *Omni*, December 1992, p. 99.

16. Carl Pfluger, "God Versus the Flying Saucers," in *Southwest Review*, September 1, 1993, p. 555, inserts added.

17. *First Contact: The Search for Extraterrestrial Intelligence*, ed. Ben Bova (New York: Nal Books, 1990), p. 58.

18. Ibid.

19. Alnor, *UFOs in New Age*, p. 17.

20. McGuire, "Alien Invaders."

21. Don Berliner and Stanton T. Friedman, *Crash at Corona: The U.S. Military Retrieval and Cover-up of a UFO* (New York: Paragon House, 1992), p. 108.

22. Linda Howe, "More Information on Cattle Mutilations," in *San Francisco Chronicle*, October 19, 1967, downloaded from Internet.

23. George Mather and Larry Nichols, *Dictionary of Cults, Sects, Religions and the Occult* (Grand Rapids: Zondervan Publishing House, 1993), p. 243. See also A. S. Ross, "Blame It on the Devil," in *Redbook*, June 1, 1994, pp. 86–87.

24. Alnor, *UFOs in New Age*, p. 39.

25. Mitch Weiss, "Thousands Try to Get a Line on Crop Circles," in *Los Angeles Times*, September 8, 1996, p. 18.

26. Michael Precker, "Meanwhile, Out in Cyberspace," in *Dallas Morning News*, June 29, 1997, p. 4F.

27. Paula Fredriksen, "Apocalypse Soon," in *National Review*, December 31, 1996, p. 34.

Chapter 1—UFOria: The Wild Popularity of UFOs

1. Gayle White, "Extraterrestrial Encounters," in *The Atlanta Journal and Constitution*, April 5, 1997, p. F04.

2. Alnor, *UFOs in New Age*, p. 73, insert added.

3. Ibid.

4. I.D.E. Thomas, *The Omega Conspiracy: Satan's Last Assault on God's Kingdom* (Oklahoma City: Hearthstone Publishing Ltd., 1986), p. 37.

5. William M. Alnor, "The Alien Obsession with Repudiating Christianity," in *SCP Journal*, 17:1–2, 1992, p. 28.

6. Cited in Brooks Alexander, "Theology from the Twilight Zone," in *Christianity Today*, September 18, 1987, p. 22.

7. Ibid.

8. Philip J. Imbrogno, "Close Encounters of the Tristate Kind," in *Spotlight*, February 1990, p. 39.

9. Russell Chandler, *Doomsday: The End of the World* (Ann Arbor, MI: Servant Publications, 1993), p. 187; cf. Hillel Schwartz, *Century's End* (New York: Doubleday, 1990), p. 260.

10. "Your Views on the UFO Phenomenon," 1997, MSNBC Home Page, downloaded from Internet.

11. Ellen Barry, "What We Believe," in *The Boston Phoenix*, August 14–21, 1997, downloaded from Internet.

12. White, "Encounters," p. F04.

13. Michael Kaplan, "Do Stars Believe in UFOs?" in *Time*, July 1, 1996, p. 27.
14. Bart Mills, "What Happened in Roswell, N.M.?" in *Los Angeles Times*, July 31, 1994, p. 6.
15. Kaplan, "Stars," p. 27.
16. Ibid.
17. "America Starry-Eyed as Space Dominates Popular Culture," in *Florida Today Space Online*, Associated Press, July 8, 1997, downloaded from Internet.
18. Dennis McLellan, "Are We Alone?" in *Los Angeles Times*, July 3, 1996, p. 1.
19. Ibid.
20. Bruce Handy, "Roswell or Bust," in *Time*, June 23, 1997, downloaded from Internet.
21. McLellan, "Alone," p. 1.
22. Waldrep, "Beam Me Up, Scotty."
23. William M. Alnor, "UFO Cults Are Flourishing in New Age Circles," in *Christian Research Journal*, Summer 1990, p. 35.
24. Alnor, "Alien Obsession," p. 32.
25. John Wiley, "Phenomena: Comment and Notes," in *The Smithsonian*, January 1983, p. 24.
26. Ibid.
27. Dana Parsons, "Looking Beyond the Heavens in Search of a Reason to Believe," in *Los Angeles Times*, July 6, 1997, p. 1.
28. Ibid.
29. Bill Hendrick, "UFOs and the Otherworldly: Do You Believe?" in *The Atlanta Journal and Constitution*, June 25, 1997, p. B01.
30. White, "Encounters," p. F04.
31. "America Starry-Eyed."
32. Associated Press, "An Age for Angels: Spiritual, Commercial Interest in Heavenly Beings on the Rise," in *Los Angeles Times*, September 19, 1992, p. 4.
33. John Ronner, quoted in Lisa Daniels, "Faithful Are Aflutter About Angels," in *San Jose Mercury News*, November 26, 1992, p. 18H.
34. Veronique de Turenne, "Taking Wing: Protection and Comfort an Angel's Breath Away," in *Orange County Register*, December 27, 1992, pp. H1, H4.
35. Stephan Salisbury, "Undeniable Financial Opportunity," in *The Philadelphia Inquirer*, July 3, 1997, downloaded from Internet.
36. McLellan, "Alone," p. 1.
37. Salisbury, "Opportunity."
38. Hendrick, "Otherwordly," p. B01.
39. Ibid.
40. Russell Chandler, *Understanding the New Age* (Dallas: Word Publishing, 1991), p. 268.
41. Charles Colson, *Kingdoms in Conflict* (New York: William Morrow, 1987), p. 78.
42. John Stott, lecture given at All Saints by the Sea Episcopal Church, Santa Barbara, California, November 14, 1987; cited in Chandler, *Understanding*, p. 268.

Chapter 2—The Search for Extraterrestrial Life

1. Frank White, *The SETI Factor* (New York: Walker and Company, 1990), p. 1.

2. Ibid, p. 35.
3. *The Gods Have Landed: New Religions from Other Worlds,* ed. James R. Lewis (New York: State University of New York Press, 1995), pp. 188–89.
4. Hendrick, "Otherworldly," p. B01.
5. Hugh Downs, "From Roswell to Our Town: Lost Out Here in the Stars," transcript of "ABC News," 1997, downloaded from Internet.
6. *First Contact: The Search for Extraterrestrial Intelligence,* ed. Ben Bova (New York: Nal Books, 1990), p. 28.
7. Isaac Asimov, "Life," in *Colliers Encyclopedia* CD-ROM, A Division of Newfield Publications, Inc.
8. Whitley Strieber, *Communion: A True Story* (New York: Beech Tree Books, 1987), p. 238.
9. Ibid.
10. Marcus Chown, "Is Anybody Out There?" in *World Press Review,* April 1997, p. 41.
11. Ibid.
12. Michael Lindemann, "SETI Scientist Describes Probable Aliens," on *CNI News,* UFO Folklore Center web site, 1997, downloaded from Internet.
13. Ibid.
14. Ibid.
15. SETI Institute, "Frequently Asked Questions," on SETI Institute web site, 2035 Landings Drive, Mountain View, CA 94043.
16. Ron Harris, "Search for Alien Life Continues," Associated Press, August 13, 1997, downloaded from Internet.
17. Thomas R. McDonough, *The Search for Extraterrestrial Intelligence* (New York: John Wiley & Sons, Inc., 1987), p. 167.
18. Ibid.
19. SETI Institute, "Questions."
20. Ibid.
21. Ibid.
22. White, *SETI Factor,* p. 8.
23. Ibid., pp. 96–99.
24. Jacques Vallee, *Revelations: Alien Contact and Human Deception* (New York: Ballantine Books, 1991), p. 230.
25. White, *SETI Factor,* pp. 133–34.
26. Berliner and Friedman, *Crash at Corona,* p. 185.
27. Ibid.
28. White, *SETI Factor,* p. 198.
29. *First Contact,* op. cit., pp. 245–46.
30. We will see later in the book that popular writer Hal Lindsey is among those who are persuaded of this possibility.
31. White, *SETI Factor,* p. 1.
32. John Winston Moore, "Review of Contact," in *SCP Newsletter,* Summer 1997, downloaded from Spiritual Counterfeits Project web site.
33. Ibid.
34. Ibid.
35. White, *SETI Factor,* pp. 113–14.
36. Ibid.

37. Ibid, p. 182.
38. Lewis, ed., *Gods Have Landed*, p. 194.
39. Ron Rhodes, *Christ Before the Manger: The Life and Times of the Preincarnate Christ* (Grand Rapids: Baker Book House, 1992), pp. 55–56.
40. Elliot Miller, "Questions and Answers," in *Christian Research Newsletter*, July/September 1992, p. 4.
41. John Calvin, *Institutes of the Christian Religion*, ed. John T. McNeill, trans. Ford Lewis Battles (Philadelphia: Westminster, 1960), I:53.
42. Miller, "Questions," p. 4.

Chapter 3—What Really Happened at Roswell?

1. Martha Mendoza, "'Aliens Actually Dummies," Associated Press, via AOL News, June 20, 1997, downloaded from Internet.
2. Interview by Charles Krause, *Jim Lehrer Show*, 1997, transcript downloaded from Internet.
3. Ibid.
4. Bruce Handy, "Roswell or Bust," in *Time*, June 23, 1997, downloaded from Internet.
5. Art Levine, "A Little Less Balance, Please," in *U.S. News and World Report*, July 14, 1997, p. 56.
6. Richard Price, "UFO Believers Find They're Not Alone," in *Florida Today*, July 3, 1997, downloaded from Internet.
7. Anne Dingus, "The New Mex Files," in *Texas Monthly*, July 1997, p. 52.
8. Brian Rooney, "People of Roswell Still Believe in UFO Story," transcript of *World News Tonight with Peter Jennings*, June 23, 1997, downloaded from Internet.
9. Matt Richtel, "A Town Braces As the Believers Descend," in the *New York Times*, July 1, 1997, downloaded from Internet.
10. Suzanne McDermott, "The Roswell Incident," in *CyberTimes*, July 7, 1997, downloaded from Internet.
11. "Roswell Alien Slime Only $2.49," CNN Interactive web site, July 3, 1997, downloaded from Internet.
12. "Postal Service Gets Aboard," in *Newsday*, June 26, 1997, p. A08.
13. Martha Mendoza, "N.M. Benefits from Alien Party," Associated Press, via AOL News, July 9, 1997, downloaded from Internet.
14. Price, "UFO Believers."
15. See the Bibliography.
16. Leon Jaroff, "Did Aliens Really Land?" in *Time*, June 23, 1997, downloaded from Internet.
17. Ibid.
18. John Hughes, "The True Believers (They Are Not Alone)," in *Orange County Register*, July 6, 1997, p. 6.
19. Charles Gibson, "Roswell Anniversary," transcript of *Good Morning America*, July 1, 1997, downloaded from Internet.
20. Mendoza, "Aliens Actually Dummies."
21. Kasper Zeuthen, "AF 'Final' UFO Report Stirs New Skepticism," in *Los Angeles Times*, June 25, 1997, p. A-1.

22. Martha Mendoza, "Roswell UFO Ranch Is Sacred Site," Associated Press, AOL News, July 5, 1997, downloaded from Internet.

23. Bart Mills, "What Happened in Roswell, N.M.?; Showtime Film Re-Examines Accounts of 1947 UFO Landing," in *Los Angeles Times*, July 31, 1994, p. 6.

24. Handy, "Roswell or Bust."

25. Ibid.

26. "Did UFO Hijack Senator?" in *The Philadelphia Daily News*, June 6, 1997, downloaded from Internet.

27. Handy, "Roswell or Bust," insert added.

28. "Letters," in *Time*, July 21, 1997, p. 6.

29. Handy, "Roswell or Bust."

30. Michael Shermer, "Perspective On Space Aliens—We See What We Believe We See," in *Los Angeles Times*, June 26, 1997, p. B-9.

31. Ibid.

32. Ibid.

33. Ibid.

34. Ibid.

35. Ibid.

36. Ibid.

37. Levine, "Less Balance," p. 56.

38. Ibid.

39. Ibid.

40. Ibid.

Chapter 4—Is There Any Hard Evidence?

1. Alan Hale, "An Astronomer's Personal Statement on UFOs," in *Skeptical Inquirer*, March-April 1997, p. 29.

2. Brooks Alexander, "Machines Made of Shadows," in *SCP Journal*, 17:1–2, 1992, p. 9.

3. John Ankerberg and John Weldon, "UFO Encounters," in *SCP Journal*, 17:1–2, 1992, p. 17.

4. Ibid.

5. Handy, "Roswell or Bust."

6. Ibid.

7. Richard Kadrey, "UFOs," in *Comptons Online Encyclopedia*, downloaded from Internet.

8. This report in particular has come under severe criticism by UFO proponents since its release.

9. Kadrey, "UFOs."

10. Kendrick Frazier, "UFOs Real? Government Covering Up?" in *Skeptical Inquirer*, November-December 1995, p. 3.

11. Ted Koppel and Jeff Greenfield, "The Making of a Myth," transcript of *Nightline*, July 4, 1997, downloaded from Internet.

12. Marshall Fine, "Many Believe There Are Men Among Us Who 'Collect' UFO Info for Government," July 3, 1997, Florida Today Space Online, downloaded from Internet.

13. Ibid.

14. Ibid.

15. Interview with Philip Klass, "Kidnapped By UFOs?" 1996, NOVA Online web site, 1997, downloaded from Internet.

16. *The UFO Phenomenon: Mysteries of the Unknown*, ed. Time-Life (Alexandria, VA: Time-Life Books, n.d), p. 104.

17. Ibid.

18. Ibid.

19. Ibid.

20. Waldrep, "Beam Me Up."

21. Ibid.

22. "Your Views on the UFO Phenomenon," MSNBC Home Page, 1997.

23. Ibid.

24. Steve Elliott, "Military Takes Blame for UFO Lights," Associated Press, July 25, 1997, downloaded from Internet.

25. Ibid.

26. Kadrey, "UFOs."

27. Howard Blum, *Out There: The Government's Secret Quest for Extraterrestrials* (New York: Simon and Schuster, 1990), p. 25.

28. Waldrep, "Beam Me Up."

29. Interview with Philip Klass, NOVA Online, insert added.

30. Hale, "Astronomer's Statement," p. 29.

31. Ibid.

32. "U.S. Lied in UFO Explanations," The Associated Press, August 2, 1997, downloaded from Internet.

33. Ibid.

34. Ibid.

35. "U.S. Feared Soviets Might Exploit UFO Sightings," in *Los Angeles Times*, August 4, 1997, p. A-4, downloaded from Internet.

36. Ibid.

37. Ibid.

38. "U.S. Lied."

Chapter 5—Are UFOs Mentioned in the Bible?

1. C. Bryan, *Close Encounters of the Fourth Kind: Alien Abduction, UFOs, and the Conference at MIT* (New York: Alfred A. Knopf, 1995), pp. 424–26.

2. Alnor, *UFOs in New Age*.

3. White, "Encounters," p. F04.

4. Richard Hall, *Uninvited Guests: A Documented History of UFO Sightings, Alien Encounters, & Cover-ups* (Santa Fe: Aurora Press, 1988), pp. 139–40.

5. *Gods Have Landed*, pp. 32–33.

6. Waldrep, "Beam Me Up."

7. *Gods Have Landed*, p. 35.

8. UFO Phenomenon, p. 12.

9. White, "Encounters," p. F04.

10. *Gods Have Landed*, p. 35.

11. Ibid., pp. 32–33.

12. Alnor, *UFOs in New Age*, pp. 222–23.
13. Ibid.
14. *Gods Have Landed*, p. 35.
15. Hall, *Uninvited*, pp. 139–40.
16. White, "Encounters," p. F04.
17. Don Berliner and Stanton T. Friedman, *Crash at Corona: The U.S. Military Retrieval and Cover-up of a UFO* (New York, NY: Paragon House, 1992), p. 187.
18. Hall, *Uninvited*, pp. 139–40.
19. Ibid.
20. I.D.E. Thomas, *The Omega Conspiracy: Satan's Last Assault on God's Kingdom* (Oklahoma City: Hearthstone Publishing, 1986), pp. 198–99.
21. White, *SETI Factor*, p. 4.
22. Bryan, *Close Encounters*, pp. 421–22.

Chapter 6—The New Age Embrace of UFOs

1. Brad Steiger, *Gods of Aquarius* (New York: Berkley Books, 1976), p. 40.
2. Alnor, *UFOs in New Age*, p. 106.
3. Cited in Antonio Huneeus, "Shirley MacLaine's Extraterrestrial Connection," in *UFO Universe*, September 1988, p. 33.
4. Douglas Groothuis, *Unmasking the New Age* (Downers Grove, IL: InterVarsity Press, 1986), p. 24.
5. See Alnor, *UFOs in New Age*, p. 106.
6. Huneeus, *Connection*, p. 32.
7. See Alnor, *UFOs in New Age*, p. 133.
8. Jacques Vallee, *Messengers of Deception: UFO Contacts and Cults* (Berkeley: And Or Press, 1979), p. 19.
9. Jacques Vallee, *The Invisible College* (New York: Dutton, 1975), pp. 3, 201, 204.
10. *Gods Have Landed*, p. 37.
11. Strieber, *Communion*, pp. 94–95.
12. Strieber; *Communion*, quoted in David Wimbush, *Something's Going On Out There* (Old Tappan, NJ: Revell, 1990), p. 48.
13. John Weldon; quoted in Ralph Rath, *The New Age: A Christian Critique* (South Bend, IN: Greenlawn Press, 1990), p. 86, insert added.
14. *Gods Have Landed*, p. 39.
15. Bob Larson, *Larson's Book of Cults* (Wheaton, IL: Tyndale House Publishers, 1983), p. 349.
16. George Mather and Larry Nichols, eds., *Dictionary of Cults, Sects, Religions, and the Occult* (Grand Rapids: Zondervan Publishing House, 1993), pp. 295–96.
17. Steiger, *Gods of Aquarius*, pp. 234–35.
18. Ibid., p. 13.
19. David Icke; quoted in Vishal Mangalwadi, *When the New Age Gets Old* (Downers Grove, IL: InterVarsity Press, 1993), p. 98.
20. Steiger, *Gods of Aquarius*, p. 40.
21. Brad Steiger, *The Fellowship* (New York: Ballantine, 1989), pp. 67–68.
22. Gabriel Green; quoted in Robb Fulcher, "Story of Spacemen Broadcast by Man," in *The Oregonian*, May 8, 1984, p. B2.

23. Steiger, *Gods of Aquarius*, p. 96.
24. Timothy Green Beckley, *Psychic and UFO Revelations in the Last Days* (New Brunswick, NJ: Inner Light Publications, 1989), p. 59.
25. Ibid., p. 61.
26. Ibid., p. 98.
27. Randall N. Baer, *Inside the New Age Nightmare* (Lafayette, LA: Huntington House, 1989), pp. 40–41.
28. Ibid., p. 146, insert added.
29. Ibid., pp. 40–41.
30. Ibid., pp. 29–30.
31. Steiger, *Gods of Aquarius*, p. 120.
32. Baer, *Nightmare*, pp. 40–41.
33. Beckley, *Revelations*, p. 35.
34. Baer, *Nightmare*, pp. 29–30.
35. Ibid., pp. 40–41.
36. Alnor, *UFOs in New Age*, p. 43.
37. William Alnor, "The Alien Obsession . . . with Repudiating Christianity," in *SCP Journal*, 17:1–2, 1992, p. 29.

Chapter 7—UFO Cults in the New Age

1. *Gods Have Landed*, p. 92.
2. Duane Noriyuki, "Age of Unarius—El Cajon Group Believes UFOs are Coming to Them in 2001," in *Los Angeles Times*, April 7, 1997, p. A-3.
3. *Gods Have Landed*, pp. 86, 88.
4. Ibid., p. 88.
5. Ibid., p. 90.
6. Ibid., pp. 90, 92.
7. For good material debunking the Atlantis myth, I point the reader to Karla Poewe-Hexham and Irving Hexham, "The 'Evidence' for Atlantis: Addressing New Age Apologetics," in *Christian Research Journal*, Summer 1989, pp. 16–19.
8. Mather and Nichols, *Dictionary*, p. 31.
9. Noriyuki, *Unarius*, p. 3.
10. Ibid., p. 3.
11. *Gods Have Landed*, pp. 90, 92.
12. Paul Hoversten, "With 2000 Near, UFO Believers Taking Off," in *USA TODAY*, March 31, 1997, p. 02A.
13. Ibid.
14. See Claude Vorilhon, *Let's Welcome Our Fathers from Space: They Created Humanity in Their Laboratories* (Tokyo: AOM Corporation, 1986).
15. "Rael: Who Is He?" from the Raelian Home Page, downloaded from the Internet, insert added.
16. "What Happened?" from the Raelian Home Page, downloaded from the Internet.
17. I should note that the Raelians are also known for their radical views on human sexuality. Though this is a part of Rael's message, I have chosen (for space considerations) not to focus on it but rather maintain primary attention on UFOs and the "Elohim."

18. "The Messages of the Elohim," Book One, Raelian Home Page, downloaded from Internet.
19. "What Happened?" op. cit.
20. "Where Do We Come From? Who Are We? Where Are We Headed?" *PR Newswire*, May 21, 1997, downloaded from Internet.
21. Elif Kaban, "Swiss Cultists Gather for Sensual Meditation," Reuters, August 6, 1997, downloaded from AR-Talk, Internet.
22. *Gods Have Landed*, p. 107. See also "Messages of Elohim."
23. "Why Do They Need an Embassy?" from the Raelian Home Page, downloaded from the Internet.
24. Ibid.
25. "Where Do We Come From?"
26. William M. Alnor, "UFO Cults Are Flourishing in New Age Circles," *Christian Research Journal*, Summer 1990, p. 35.
27. Aetherius Society Home Page (Internet).
28. *The Watchman Expositor*, 1997–1998 Index of Cults and Religions, Watchman Fellowship, vol. 14 no. 3, p. 4.
29. Sidney Jansma, UFOs and Evolution (1981), pp. 77–78.
30. "The Aetherius Society: A Cosmic Concept," Aetherius Society home page (Internet).
31. Mather and Nichols, *Dictionary*, p. 15.
32. Jansma, *UFOs and Evolution*, pp. 77–78.
33. Mather and Nichols, *Dictionary*, p. 15.
34. "The Aetherius Society: A Cosmic Concept."
35. Ibid.
36. Ibid.
37. Mather and Nichols, *Dictionary*, p. 15.
38. Jansma, *UFOs and Evolution*, pp. 77–78.
39. Aetherius Society home page (Internet).
40. Ibid.
41. Ibid.
42. Ibid.
43. Ibid.
44. Jansma, *UFOs and Evolution*, pp. 77–78.
45. Ibid.
46. Ibid.
47. Paul McGuire, "Alien Invaders," in *Charisma* magazine web site, 1997, downloaded from Internet.
48. Gretchen Passantino, "The Heaven's Gate Cult," Answers in Action web site, 1997, downloaded from Internet.
49. Ibid.
50. Ibid.
51. "Heaven's Gate: Our Position Against Suicide," Heaven's Gate web site, 1997, downloaded from Internet.
52. Noah Robischon, Cathy Booth, James Willwerth, Nancy Harbert, Rachele Kanigal, and Richard N. Ostling, "Planet Earth About to Be Recycled," in *Time*, 1997, downloaded from Internet.

53. Passantino, Answers in Action web site.
54. Douglas Groothuis, "Making Sense of Heaven's Gate," in *Apologia Report*, 1997, downloaded from Internet.

Chapter 8—The Occult Connection

1. Jansma, *UFOs and Evolution*, p. 92.
2. See Alnor, *UFOs in New Age*, p. 76.
3. John Ankerberg and John Weldon, "UFO Encounters," in *SCP Journal*, 17:1–2, 1992, p. 16.
4. Brooks Alexander, "Machines Made of Shadows," in *SCP Journal*, 17:1–2, 1992, p. 11.
5. John Weldon with Zola Levitt, *UFOs: What on Earth Is Happening?* (Irvine, CA: Harvest House Publishers, 1975), p. 101.
6. Alnor, *UFOs in New Age*, p. 238.
7. Douglas Groothuis, *Confronting the New Age* (Downers Grove, IL: InterVarsity Press, 1988), p. 30.
8. Mather and Nichols, *Dictionary*, p. 182.
9. Ibid., p. 84.
10. Elliot Miller, *A Crash Course on the New Age Movement* (Grand Rapids: Baker Book House, 1990), p. 141.
11. Mather and Nichols, *Dictionary*, p. 31.
12. Ibid., p. 86.
13. Ibid., p. 175.
14. David Wimbish, *Something's Going On out There* (Old Tappan, NJ: Revell, 1990), p. 158.
15. Ibid., p. 158.
16. Dave Hunt, *The Cult Explosion* (Eugene, OR: Harvest House Publishers, 1978), p. 19.
17. Jansma, *UFOs and Evolution*, p. 92.
18. Jacques Vallee, *UFO Chronicles of the Soviet Union* (New York: Ballantine Books, 1992), p. 109.
19. Ibid., p. 118.
20. Ibid.
21. Alnor, *UFOs in New Age*, p. 204.
22. Ibid.
23. *Gods Have Landed*, p. 27.
24. Karla Poewe and Irving Hexham, "UFO Religion," in *Christian Century*, May 7, 1997, p. 439.
25. *Gods Have Landed*, p. 4.
26. Ibid., p. 6.
27. "Does the Bible Offer Any Clues Regarding the Significance of UFOs?" Grand Rapids: RBC Ministries, downloaded from Internet.
28. Vishal Mangalwadi, *When the New Age Gets Old* (Downers Grove, IL: InterVarsity Press, 1992), p. 87.

Chapter 9—"Alien" Abductions: Terror from the Sky

1. "Close encounter," in *National Review*, July 10, 1995, p. 26.
2. *Gods Have Landed*, p. 66.

3. Gleick James, "Human Encounters with Aliens (Book Review)," in *The New Republic*, May 30, 1994, p. 31.
4. Gayle White, "Culting of America," in *The Atlanta Journal and Constitution*, September 30, 1995, p. E/06. This poll has come under severe criticism from the scientific community as being invalid.
5. *Gods Have Landed*, p. 70.
6. C. Bryan, *Close Encounters of the Fourth Kind: Alien Abduction, UFOs, and the Conference at MIT* (New York: Alfred A. Knopf, 1995), pp. 17–19.
7. Ibid.
8. *Gods Have Landed*, p. 70.
9. Ibid
10. Bryan, *Close Encounters*, pp. 17–19.
11. Andrew Stuttaford, "Close Encounters of the Fourth Kind: Alien Abduction, UFOs, and the Conference at MIT," in *National Review*, September 11, 1995, p. 66.
12. Richard Hall, *Uninvited Guests: A Documented History of UFO Sightings, Alien Encounters, and Cover-ups* (Santa Fe: Aurora Press, 1988), p. 83.
13. *Gods Have Landed*, p. 69.
14. Ibid
15. Mangalwadi, *New Age Gets Old*, p. 87.
16. Bryan, *Close Encounters*, p. 40.
17. Ibid.
18. John Mack, *Abduction: Human Encounters with Aliens* (New York: Charles Scribner's Sons, 1994), p. 412.
19. Bryan, *Close Encounters*, p. 149.
20. James, "Human Encounters," p. 31, insert added.
21. Mack, *Abductions*, p. 39.
22. *Gods Have Landed*, p. 75.
23. James, "Human Encounters," p. 31.
24. Mack, *Abductions*, p. 102.
25. Ibid., p. 271.
26. Ibid., p. 131.
27. Ibid., pp. 407–08.
28. Ibid., p. 8.
29. Bryan, *Close Encounters*, p. 143.
30. Ibid.
31. *Gods Have Landed*, p. 76.
32. Ibid.
33. Jacques Vallee, *Confrontations: A Scientist's Search for Alien Contact* (New York: Ballantine, 1990), p. 17.
34. Ibid.
35. *Gods Have Landed*, p. 77.
36. Fannie Weinstein, "Have Some of Us Encountered Aliens?" Gannett News Service, April 26, 1994, downloaded from Internet.
37. Waldrep, "Beam Me Up."
38. James, "Human Encounters," p. 31.
39. Stuttaford, "Close Encounters," p. 66.
40. Weinstein, "Encountered."

41. Ibid., insert added.
42. Bryan, *Close Encounters*, pp. 259–66.
43. Ibid.
44. Jill Neimark, "The Harvard professor and the UFOs," in *Psychology Today*, March-April 1994, p. 46.
45. James, "Human Encounters," p. 31.
46. Mack, *Abduction*, p. 76.
47. Ibid., p. 178.
48. Ibid., p. 202.
49. Ibid.
50. Ibid., pp. 265–67, 283.
51. Wing-Tsit Chan, translator and compiler, *A Source Book in Chinese Philosophy* (Princeton: Princeton University Press, 1963), p. 136.
52. *Tao-te Ching*, pp. 1, 4, 14, 21; cf. Herlee G. Creel, *Chinese Thought from Confucius to Mao Tse-Tung* (Chicago: University of Chicago Press, 1953), pp. 101–02.
53. David Chow and Richard Spangler, *Kung Fu: History, Philosophy and Technique* (Hollywood: Unique Publications Company, 1980), pp. 16–17; cf. *Tao-te Ching*, p. 42.
54. Donn F. Draeger and Robert W. Smith, *Comprehensive Asian Fighting Arts* (Tokyo: Kodansha International, 1980), pp. 16, 31–33.
55. Stephen Schumacher and Gert Woerner, eds., *The Encyclopedia of Eastern Philosophy and Religion* (Boston: Shambhala Publications, 1989), p. 358.
56. Charles Holcombe, "The Taoist Origins of the Chinese Martial Arts," in *Journal of Asian Martial Arts*, January 1993, p. 13. Chi is understood to be the energy and matter produced by the interaction between yin and yang (see John P. Painter, "Will the Real Yin and Yang Please Stand Up?" in *Inside Kung-Fu*, December 1991, pp. 39–42).
57. Chow and Spangler, *Kung Fu*, pp. 24–25.
58. Mack, *Abduction*, pp. 265–67, 283.
59. Ibid.
60. Neimark, "Harvard Professor," p. 46.
61. Stuttaford, "Close Encounters," p. 66.
62. Ibid.
63. Neimark, "Harvard Professor," p. 46.
64. James, "Human Encounters," p. 31.
65. Ibid.
66. Neimark, "Harvard Professor," p. 46.
67. Bryan, *Close Encounters*, pp. 144–45.
68. Stuttaford, "Close Encounters," p. 66.
69. Mangalwadi, *New Age Gets Old*, p. 96.
70. Ibid.
71. *Gods Have Landed*, p. 68.
72. Ibid.

Chapter 10—The Strange Case of Whitley Strieber

1. Keith Thompson, *Angels and Aliens: UFOs and the Mythic Imagination* (New York: Addison-Wesley Publishing Co., 1954), pp. 202–03.

2. Strieber, *Communion,* p. 57.
3. Thompson, *Angels and Aliens,* pp. 202–03.
4. Strieber, *Communion,* pp. 28–30.
5. Ibid., p. 30.
6. See Wimbish, *Something's Going On,* p. 16.
7. See Alnor, "UFO Cults Are Flourishing," p. 5.
8. See Wimbish, *Something's Going On,* p. 16.
9. Tal Brooke, *When the World Will Be As One* (Eugene, OR: Harvest House Publishers, 1989), pp. 24–26.
10. Ibid.
11. Ibid.
12. Strieber, *Communion,* p. 26.
13. Whitley Strieber, *Transformation: The Breakthrough* (New York: Avon, 1989), p. 69.
14. See Alnor, *UFOs in New Age,* pp. 100–01.
15. Philip J. Klass, "UFO-Abductions: Dangerous Games," in *Not Necessarily the New Age,* ed. Robert Basil (Buffalo: Prometheus Books, 1988), p. 221.
16. See Alnor, "UFO Cults Are Flourishing," p. 5.
17. Strieber, *Communion,* pp. 114–15.
18. Ibid., p. 274.
19. Strieber, *Communion;* quoted in Alnor, *UFOs in the New Age,* p. 105.
20. Alnor, "UFO Cults Are Flourishing," p. 35.
21. Strieber, *Transformation,* p. 52.
22. Ibid., pp. 227–28.
23. Ibid., p. 11.
24. Ibid.

Chapter 11—Demonized Delusions in the End Times

1. Official policy statement found in *Flying Saucer Review* descriptive brochure, 1992 (Flying Saucer Review, P.O. Box 162, High Wycombe, Bucks, HP13 5D2 England); cited in Ankerberg and Weldon, "UFO Encounters," p. 20.
2. Mark Albrecht; quoted in Ralph Rath, *The New Age: A Christian Critique* (South Bend, IN: Greenlawn Press, 1990), p. 83.
3. Ankerberg and Weldon, "UFO Encounters," p. 21, italics added.
4. Rath, *New Age,* p. 84.
5. David Wimbish, *Something's Going On,* p. 46.
6. Ibid.
7. Weldon with Levitt, *UFOs: What on Earth,* p. 101; Alnor "UFO Cults Are Flourishing," p. 5.
8. Paul McGuire, "Alien Invaders," in *Charisma* magazine web site, 1997, downloaded from Internet.
9. Brooks Alexander; quoted by Randall Baer, *Inside the New Age Nightmare* (Lafayette, LA: Huntington House, 1989), p. 108.
10. John Keel, *UFOs: Operation Trojan Horse* (New York: G.P. Putnam's Sons, 1970), pp. 215, 299.
11. Cited in Hal Lindsey, *Planet Earth—2000 A.D.* (Palos Verdes, CA: Western Front, 1994), pp. 72–75.

12. Ibid.
13. Vallee, *Messengers*, p. 15.
14. Vallee, *Confrontations*, pp. 160–61.
15. Lynn E. Catoe; cited in I.D.E. Thomas, *The Omega Conspiracy* (Oklahoma City: Hearthstone Publishing Ltd., 1986), p. 73.
16. Baer, *Nightmares*, p. 109.
17. Waldrep, "Beam Me Up."
18. "Spiritual Warfare? Some Look to Bible for Answers to Alien Abductions," in *Florida Today*, August 17, 1997, downloaded from Internet.
19. Ibid.
20. Steiger, *Gods of Aquarius*, p. 6.
21. Keel, *Trojan Horse*, p. 143.
22. Keith Thompson, *Angels and Aliens: UFOs and the Mythic Imagination* (New York: Addison-Wesley Publishing Co., 1954), p. 124.
23. Ibid.
24. Ibid.
25. Ibid., p. 186.
26. Gayle White, "Extraterrestrial Encounters," in *Atlanta Journal and Constitution*, April 5, 1997, p. F04.
27. Merrill F. Unger, *Demons in the World Today* (Wheaton: Tyndale House Publishers, 1971), pp. 44–45.
28. "Spiritual Warfare? Some Look to Bible."
29. Ibid.
30. Ibid.
31. Ibid.
32. Ibid.
33. Ibid.
34. J. Allen Hynek, *The UFO Experience: A Scientific Inquiry* (Chicago: Henry Regnery Company, 1972), p. 201.
35. Scott Smith, "There's a Bigger Universe out There Than Meets the Eye—Or Telescope," in *The Business Journal*, 1997, downloaded from Internet.
36. Mack, *Abduction*, p. 10.
37. Ibid., p. 11.
38. Jacques Vallee, *UFO Chronicles of the Soviet Union* (New York: Ballantine Books, 1992), p. 33.
39. Hall, *Uninvited Guests*, p. 125.
40. Vallee, *UFO Chronicles*, p. 39.
41. Hall, *Uninvited Guests*, pp. 127–29.
42. Benjamin Creme, *The Reappearance of the Christ and the Masters of Wisdom* (Los Angeles: The Tara Press, 1980), p. 207.
43. Ron Rhodes, *The Counterfeit Christ of the New Age Movement* (Grand Rapids: Baker Book House, 1990), p. 245.
44. Timothy Green Beckley, *Psychic and UFO Revelations in the Last Days* (New Brunswick, NJ: Inner Light Publications, 1989), pp. 74–75.
45. McGuire, "Alien Invaders."
46. "Spiritual Warfare? Some Look to Bible," op. cit
47. Ibid.

48. Online Bible.
49. Lindsey, *Planet Earth—2000 A.D.*, p. 78.
50. Ibid., pp. 68–69.
51. McGuire, "Alien Invaders."
52. Gleason Archer, *The Encyclopedia of Bible Difficulties* (Grand Rapids: Zondervan Publishing House, 1982), p. 80.

Chapter 12—The Rise of Doomsday Shivers

1. Ted Daniels, press release, Millennium Watch Institute, downloaded from MWI web site.
2. Steiger, *Gods of Aquarius*, p. 40.
3. Paula Fredriksen, "Apocalypse Soon," in *National Review*, December 31, 1996, p. 34.
4. Stephen D. O'Leary, "Heaven's Gate and the Culture of Popular Millennialism," Center for Millennial Studies, April 1997, downloaded from CMW web site.
5. Ned Potter and Peter Jennings, "Coming Millennium Triggers Fears Among Cult Groups," transcript of *World News Tonight with Peter Jennings*, American Broadcasting Companies, Inc., March 27, 1997.
6. Lee Krenis, "More, Millennium Or Media?" Gannett News Service, May 23, 1994, downloaded from Internet.
7. Richard Landes, "Countdown 2000," Center for Millennial Studies, 1997, downloaded from CMS web site.
8. Charles Berlitz, *Doomsday 1999 A.D.* (New York: Doubleday & Company, 1981), p. 9.
9. Based on Charles Berlitz and Frederick H. Marten, *The Story of Human Life*; cited in Stanley Young, "An Overview of the End," in *Critique*, vol. 31 (1989):65.
10. For example, Bill Lawren, "Are You Ready for Millennial Fever?" in *Utne Reader*, March/April 1990; Young, "Overview," pp. 28–31; and Berlitz, *Doomsday*.
11. Note that most of the accounts of the turbulence and panic that accompanied the arrival of A.D. 1000 come indirectly from the *Histories* of Raoul Glaber, a Burgundian monk born in the late tenth century.
12. Russell Chandler, *Doomsday: The End of the World* (Ann Arbor, MI: Servant Publications, 1993), p. 54.
13. Ibid., p. 52.
14. Yuri Rubinsky and Ian Wiseman, *A History of the End of the World* (New York: William Morrow and Co., 1982), p. 66.
15. Chandler, *Doomsday*, p. 54.
16. Ibid.
17. Louis Berkhof, *The History of Christian Doctrines* (Grand Rapids: Baker Book House, 1981), p. 263.
18. Philip Schaff, *History of the Christian Church*, vol. 2, p. 348.
19. Stanley J. Grenz, *The Millennial Maze: Sorting Out Evangelical Options* (Downers Grove, IL: InterVarsity Press, 1992), p. 14.
20. Ibid., p. 44.
21. Henri Focillon, *The Year 1000* (New York: Frederick Ungar Publishing Co., n.d.), p. 59.

22. Ibid., p. 60.
23. Grenz, *Millennial Maze*, p. 19.
24. Ibid., p. 22.
25. Lawren, "Are You Ready?" p. 96.
26. Potter and Jennings, "Coming Millennium."
27. David Spangler, *Emergence: The Rebirth of the Sacred* (New York: Dell, 1984), p. 19.
28. John Dart, "Sect Leader Continues to Spread Word Despite Uproar Over Forecasts," in *Los Angeles Times*, February 23, 1991, p. F20.
29. See Ron Rhodes, "What's New in the Headlines," in *Christian Research Newsletter* 3:3, p. 6.
30. Timothy Egan, "Guru's Bomb Shelter Hits Legal Snag," in *New York Times*, April 24, 1990, p. A8.
31. Hugh Downs, "From Roswell to Our Town: Lost Out Here in the Stars," *ABC News*, downloaded from Internet, 1997.
32. Aaron M. Katz, "Heaven's Gate: A Harbinger of Things to Come?" Center for Millennial Studies, 1997, downloaded from CMS web site.
33. Kenneth Siber and Don Whipple, "Alien Invaders Stir Earthly Imaginations," *Insight on the News*, July 15, 1996, p. 40.
34. Jacques Vallee, *Revelations: Alien Contact and Human Deception* (New York: Ballantine Books, 1991), p. 228.
35. *Gods Have Landed*, p. 41.

Chapter 13—Against the Darkness

1. Norman Geisler and William Watkins, *Worlds Apart: A Handbook on World Views* (Grand Rapids: Baker Book House, 1989), p. 11.

Appendix A—Who Is Satan?

1. C. Fred Dickason, *Angels, Elect and Evil* (Chicago: Moody Press, 1978), p. 122.
2. Charles Hodge, *Systematic Theology*, ed. Edward N. Gross (Grand Rapids: Baker Book House, 1988), p. 235.
3. Ray C. Stedman, *Spiritual Warfare* (Waco: Word Books, 1976), p. 22.
4. Henry C. Thiessen, *Lectures in Systematic Theology* (Grand Rapids: Eerdmans, 1981), p. 142.
5. Lewis Sperry Chafer; cited in Thomas Ice and Robert Dean, *A Holy Rebellion* (Eugene, OR: Harvest House, 1990), p. 60.
6. Thiessen, *Lectures*, p. 142.
7. Ice and Dean, *Holy Rebellion*, p. 46.

Appendix B—Who Are Demons?

1. This is the view of Paul Enns, *The Moody Handbook of Theology* (Chicago: Moody Press, 1989), p. 294.
2. See Charles C. Ryrie, *Basic Theology* (Wheaton: Victor Books, 1986), p. 159.
3. Merrill F. Unger; cited in Henry Clarence Thiessen, *Lectures in Systematic Theology* (Grand Rapids: Eerdmans, 1981), p. 141.

4. Unger, *Demons*, p. 28.
5. Millard J. Erickson, *Christian Theology* (Grand Rapids: Baker Book House, 1987), p. 450.
6. Ryrie, *Theology*, p. 159, insert mine; cf. Unger, *Demons*, pp. 15–16.
7. See Ryrie, *Theology*, p. 159; cf. Clinton E. Arnold, *Powers of Darkness: Principalities and Powers in Paul's Letters* (Downers Grove, IL: InterVarsity Press, 1992), pp. 65–67.
8. Charles C. Ryrie, *You Mean the Bible Teaches That?* (Chicago: Moody Press, 1976), p. 99.
9. Enns, *Handbook*, p. 297.

Appendix C—The Christian's Defense Against Fallen Angels

1. See, for example, Ice and Dean, *Holy Rebellion*, Chapter 8.
2. Ray C. Stedman, *Spiritual Warfare* (Waco: Word Books, 1976), p. 114.
3. Erickson, *Theology*, p. 449.